AUSTRALIA - What is it?

AUSTRALIA— What is it?

HENRY WILLIAMS

Illustrated by Paul Rigby

seal books

RIGBY

Rigby Limited, Adelaide • Sydney • Melbourne
Brisbane • Perth

First published 1971
Published in Seal Books 1973
Copyright © 1971 H. Williams
Library of Congress Catalog Card Number 74-141715
National Library of Australia Card Number
& ISBN 0 85179 281 2
All rights reserved

Printed in Hong Kong

CONTENTS

1	History and Origins	1
2	The Political Line-up	19
3	The Economic Mix-up	33
4	The Social Set-up	50
5	The Culture Hang-up	70
6	The Mystique Fog-up	95
7	The Future	108

1

HISTORY AND ORIGINS

In 1788, when white men first took up permanent residence on the shores of Australia, the American War of Independence had been over for five years.

A year later, in 1789, the street mobs of Paris would storm the Bastille, the crumbling mediaeval church and chateau fastnesses of Europe would be torn asunder, and the cries of "*Liberté! Égalité! Fraternité!*" would herald the Age of the Common Man.

It would be seventy-two years before Burke and Wills made it to the north coast, seventy-three years before the first Melbourne Cup was run, ninety-five years before the Ashes stayed Down Under, 112 years before the six Australian states federated, and 166 years before an Aussie ran a four-minute mile.

But, to get back to the beginning. The name that comes instantly to mind in association with the discovery of Australia is Captain Cook, and is, of course, not strictly accurate.

The Dutch had been around in the East Indies long before Cook arrived on the scene. Dutch navigators had charted the coast from Cape York right around to the west. Charted it, but nothing more. They had the dykes and the windmills and the tulip fields of Holland to go back to; they were unfamiliar with the great Australian imperative: "Give it a go." To be shipwrecked on such a barren coastline would be bad enough; to settle there voluntarily was unthinkable.

It was left to a later generation of non-Dutch settlers to wish that they had. In the words of an itinerant ringer last seen reflecting over a schooner of beer in a pub in Marble Bar, "If this earth were shaped like a cow, this country up here would be its arse-end."

Nowhere, in fact, does one have such an overwhelming sensation of being out on the edge of nowhere, such an intuitive conviction of the reality of nothing, as in the far north-west

There is a lunar-like remoteness about those riven and

blistered landscapes: so much so that it has been said that should any moonbound astronauts, by some inadvertent navigational error, land anywhere behind Carnarvon, Broome, Wyndham or Derby they might well emerge from their spacecraft and look around with every conviction that they had arrived at their destination. (See *North-west Australia — Why Is It There?* Professor C. Block. University of Australasia Press.)

We may say then, with as much certainty as one can ever say anything in these matters, that it was the lunar desolation of the north-western perimeter that determined the

form Australia was to take; that made it eventually New South Wales and not New Holland.

Why, incidentally, the name of New South Wales for a land that was to attract far more Irishmen and Scotsmen than ever it did Welshmen?

Admittedly, the name New England had already been used in North America. But why not New Scotland or New Ireland?

Was it that the strip of the Pacific Ocean outside Sydney Harbour reminded someone of the Bristol Channel? Or was it that the natives of South Wales, which in later industrial depressions was to produce more communists, anarchists, failed poets and intellectual malcontents per acre than any other spot in the United Kingdom, with the possible exceptions of Oxford and Cambridge, were already regarded as a lawless and turbulent lot, and it was hoped that this new faraway land would attract them? Or was it that a Permanent Second Secretary in the Colonial Office had a married sister living in Cardiff or something of that nature? The official story is that the landscape reminded Captain Cook of that of South Wales, which makes one suspect that, however well he knew his way around the Pacific, he had not travelled much in the Old Country west of the Severn.

In 1770 Cook discovered the comparatively fertile and well-watered eastern seaboard and thought it land worth claiming.

True, there were occupants there already; wretched unclothed illiterate blackfellows who, most important, were virtually without armaments. But those were the days of empire-building, which was something the Aborigines knew nothing about.

They lived a simple nomadic life of food gathering within traditionally defined tribal areas. They had no roads, no fences, no cities, no written legal constitution, and, as far as one can gather, no inclination to muscle in on each other's hunting grounds as defined by immemorial custom.

They lacked dynamism, drive, ambition; they knew nothing of organised warfare, they were not aggressive, and were obviously destined to be a back number in the modern world as it was then taking shape.

There has been much debate among scholars as to how these simple people came to be in this far-flung corner of the earth in the first place.

They had no boats to speak of, they knew nothing of navigation, but they were a long, long way from that fertile valley in the Middle East or wherever it was that mankind is supposed to have originated.

Negroid in colouring, but more Caucasoid in feature, they did not fit into the established classifications; so anthropologists coined the name Australoid to bring them into the scheme of things.

This could be shirking the issue, though, as Professor Marcus Merryweather, Head of the Faculty of Anthropological Conjecture at A.N.U. has pointed out in his brilliant work, *Man—How Come?* (U. of A. Press) in which he contends that the Australoid is, in fact, the common ancestor of the Negroid and the Caucasoid, that the original Garden of Eden was probably located somewhere north of the Macdonnel Ranges, and that there was an oceanic migration in pre-historic times that sews it all up.

In support of his thesis, Professor Merryweather intends essaying a journey by gumwood raft from Western Australia to the Persian Gulf, making use of prevailing currents in the Indian Ocean, and the Department of Native Affairs has shown some interest in the project.

There is little likelihood, however, of an Aboriginal taking part in the proposed expedition, as the Aborigines, unlike later waves of Australians, have never been beset by doubts as to who they were. Most of the literature on the subject of the search for an Australian National Identity, in fact, has been written in the last fifteen years—coincidental with the introduction of television—and may possibly be related to that phenomenon. (See *Television and Reality*, Rodney Rule, Reader in Sociology, U. of Aust.)

Meanwhile, the renowned Talgai skull found by a stockman in the Darling Downs seems to point to an affinity between the early Australian Aboriginal and Java Man, and if this is confirmed with finds by other stockmen, it will call for yet another orientation in anthropological thinking.

Be that as it may, these matters did not trouble Captain Cook in his journey of discovery along the eastern seaboard.

Most men who lead adventurous lives do not have adventurous minds. They tend to be practical, competent, self-reliant, addicted to regular shaving or beard-trimming and routine checking of provisions. They do not let themselves go; they keep their minds on the job of getting to whatever far-flung destination they are making for.

Men whose minds range the frontiers of human knowledge generally have it made in cosy book-lined rooms close to museums and libraries, and often experience great difficulty in mastering such practical everyday minutiae as mending electric fuses or boiling an egg.

Cook, it would appear, ran true to type. Methodical, disciplined, down-to-earth; a man who knew where he was going, or, if he did not, was determined to find out.

Did he, as he made his epic journey of discovery along this virgin coast, wonder at all on what was to follow; the teeming metropolis of Sydney, the Point Bennelong Opera House, the great industrial complexes of Woollongong and Newcastle, the bikini-and-motel splendours of Surfers Paradise?

Probably not. When not absorbed with pencil and sextant around the binnacle, he was more likely worrying about the state of the salt pork and the lime water; looking for weevils in the flour and any signs of scurvy among the crew.

On 21 August 1770, at Possession Island off Cape York, he proclaimed this land as henceforth coming under the say-so of the Old Country — George III, to be precise — and set sail for home.

There were none to argue with this proclamation.

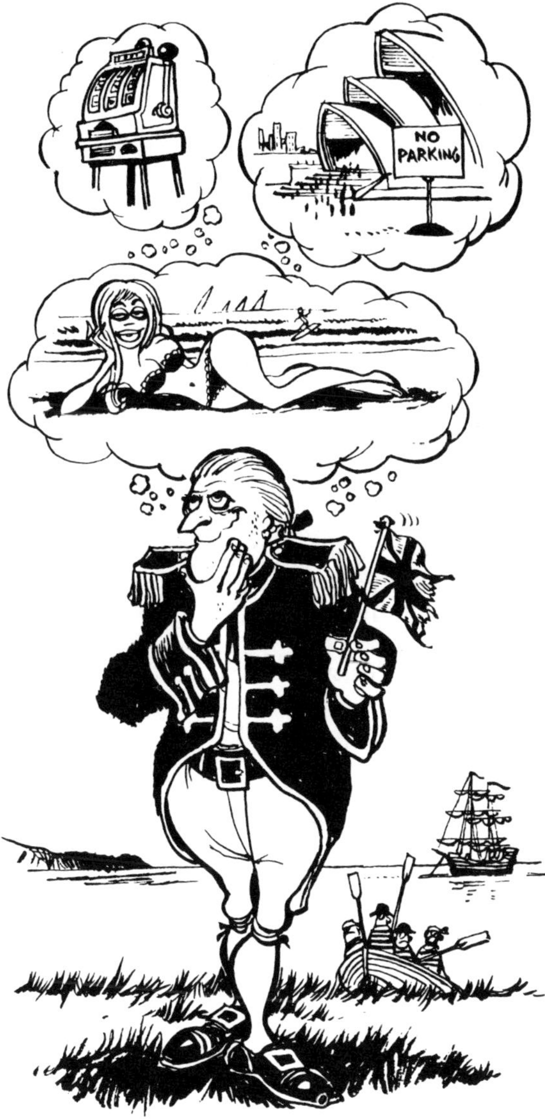
NO PARKING

The Aborigines went on hunting for goannas and witchety grubs and minding their own business. They were not to know that the reign of "big boss white fella" was under way.

It was not known then, and was not to be realised until some years after colonisation had begun, that this was the other side of the same place that the Dutch had charted in the previous century; the fabled Terra Australis that thinkers on such subjects had long conjectured must be there somewhere down under.

Nothing more was done about it for some seventeen years, when someone in faraway misty London had the bright idea that this distant land would be an ideal dumping place for the surplus convict population.

In what particular mind, at what particular time the hour strikes for those ideas that give the wheels of history a perceptible shove is a fascinating exercise for students of the mechanics of power.

Let us imagine two influential members of the English eighteenth century establishment, seated at a window in one of those exclusive clubs along the Mall, snuff-boxes and port decanter to hand:

"I was down at Portsmouth last week."

"Oh really?"

"Something must be done about those convict hulks. We won't be able to get many more into them."

"There'll be more knaves and felons than honest men about, the way things are going."

"We've got to get some of them away somewhere. Those damned American colonials won't take them any more, now they're independent."

"Send enough gunboats, they'll have to take 'em."

"It's no good Marmaduke. You're living in the past. We can't act like that any more. We lost that war, y'know."

"We should never have let the Navy Estimates slide like we did."

"I've got an idea."

"Eh?"

"Remember that Cook fellow?"

"Cook. One of the Bedfordshire Cooks, was it?"

"No, no. The sailor fellow. North Country chap. No family to speak of. Captain Cook."

"Oh, the fellow who discovered that place down under?"

"Quite!"

"Eh? You mean . . ."

"Exactly. It's far enough away. There's plenty of space there, by all accounts."

"Do you think they'd be able to find the place again?"

"I don't see why not. That Cook chappie was a first-rate navigator. He made charts and everything."

"Zounds, Arbuthnot—what a brilliant idea! I'll have a word with old whatsit at the Admiralty. See if they can lay on the transport. Let's have another port . . ."

However it was, on 26 January 1788, the First Fleet of eleven ships, with its assorted cargo of felons and jailers, sailed into Sydney Cove.

Without any choice about coming out, and none about going back, the founding fathers of white Australia had

9

arrived: the rejects of society, cast off literally to the ends of the earth.

The most exciting thing about contemporary Australia, according to many, is its future; the last continent left where the frontiers still beckon, still promise. But it was not always so.

In the early days, in fact, it was touch and go whether the place had any future at all; whether it was not one of those gigantic historical mistakes initiated by men with powerful pens behind big desks in remote seats of power.

Conscript gangs of convict labour do not leave much behind in the way of memoirs, reflections, *belles-lettres*; and it is extremely doubtful, even if they had had the time, the ink, the paper and the wherewithal to express themselves, whether what they had to say would have been fit for publication.

The grass was not so green here, the trees were not so shady; the soil was thin; the rain did not fall as it should.

The primitive way of living of the Aborigines was not entirely due to their lack of agricultural know-how. Later men, equipped with tractors and fertilisers and the profound advice of all the brains engaged in the Commonwealth Scientific and Industrial Research Organisation, were to be hard put to it to scratch a living from this unyielding earth; were oft to feel sorely tempted to throw it all in and go walkabout.

For this was a land where there were no easy pickings; where the wallabies were waiting to eat any plant that the sun did not shrivel.

Cows and horses and sheep and poultry were unknown here. Much of the livestock shipped out with the settlers had perished on the voyage; what was left was in no prime condition.

What the early settlement needed desperately, apart from stonemasons, carpenters and the like, was men who knew about seed and soil and seasons. What it had was the sweepings of the jails, largely city-bred, for whom a horse must have been something that pulled a carriage rather than a plough, and bossed over by a soldiery whose training and conditioning were for a way of life which was the complete antithesis of useful constructive toil.

And yet, in the teeth of it all, the settlement survived; it came on. Why?

There was one factor going for it that was to outweigh all the hardships, all the drawbacks; it was that home was now 12,000 miles away, and there were no return tickets.

Right from the start, the transportations included a number of womenfolk, and within a few years there was a generation of Australian-born, for whom home was here under the Southern Cross, not some misty land far over the sea.

This one-way ticket syndrome, however, has continued as a highly important factor in the settlement of Australia ever since.

Settlers arrive to this day with disturbing memories of snow and holly at Christmas, meadows and hedgerows and country lanes and drizzling rain and huddled crumbling old buildings caked with homely soot, and wonder to themselves just what they are doing in this empty sunburnt continent.

Without the fare back, however, they have to make the best of it, and stay on to find their children growing up into Aussies; men who walk barefoot over sticks and stones without saying "Ouch," who actually enjoy steak for breakfast, who do not feel it is odd to be snoozing in the sun on Christmas Day, and who do not know what "these whingeing pommy bastards" are going on about.

As there was no getting out of the place, the only thing was to go into it, and the miserable prison without bars around Sydney Cove was gradually transformed into a continent with expanding frontiers.

Men were arriving who did not have to; free settlers, looking for a better life.

In 1813 a pass was found through the Blue Mountains. Tales came back of limitless grazing pastures beyond the ranges, for the taking for men with the get up and go spirit.

The horizons were open; there were no notices saying

"Trespassers Will Be Prosecuted: and in the mushrooming pastoral bonanza that followed it looked as though this was going to develop into a land largely inhabited by sheep, with just an occasional biped in a hard-brimmed hat riding around looking after them; a picture of Australia that still obtains in certain sophisticated circles in north-west Europe.

And even among contemporary sheep graziers, who must be aware that a fair number of Australians actually live on bus routes now and make a living going into factories and offices every day, there persists a body of opinion that if you were to take the sheep out of Australia the country would immediately collapse and the inhabitants thereof would have no choice but to return to their countries of origin.

In a recent address to the Australian Wool Board entitled "The National Debt And The Merino Fleece", a leading western pastoralist expressed himself thus: "If sheep had been given the vote, the government would never have allowed wool prices to fall to the level they are today."

In the first half of the last century Britain was in the throes of the Industrial Revolution. Nylon, orlon and drip-dry shirts were unknown. Japan was still wrapped in a sort of Madam Butterfly pre-industrial torpor.

Those were the halcyon years for British manufactured goods. The textile mills of Yorkshire could not get enough wool and the quest for new pastures surged outwards; west and north and south.

This free-for-all scramble was not condoned by the authorities.

Governments, after all, stand for law and order, for not letting men do as they please. ("The essence of good government is to see that a free-for-all can never happen." See K. O. Sugg, *The Philosophy of Public Administration*.)

In 1829, Governor Sir Ralph Darling declared a boundary some 250 miles out from Sydney, beyond which it was illegal for any man to take over pastures for his stock simply because he was there.

It was one thing, however, to draw a line on a map in a Sydney office, and quite another to enforce this ordinance out back o' the Great Divide, especially when there were no police stations, town council chambers, or lawyers' offices farther out than Parramatta. A goodly proportion of Australian sheep were soon munching illegal fodder.

A few years later, another Governor bowed to the inevitable and declared it quite in order for a man to graze his stock wherever he could find feed as long as he had a "squatter's licence" — £10 per annum.

Gradually, haphazardly, without any fanfares of trumpets, the frontiers were pushed backwards.

It was a life for the hardy and self-reliant, the only link with civilization being the creaking wagons driven by the hard-swearing, hard-living bullockies, bringing up stores and taking back the wool.

Some men, known as "hatters," were driven round the bend by the monumental isolation; although it is held in some quarters today that there are now far more hatters in the corridors of Canberra than there ever were outback in the early days, only they are not called hatters any more.

In 1836, an official exploring party reached the south coast around Port Phillip Bay, to find a couple of squatters already there without the government knowing anything about it. These two, had they but known it, had founded the State of Victoria.

They had crossed over from Van Diemen's Land, later known as Tassy, where, by the living space standards of the early pastoralists, things were already a bit over-crowded.

There were rich grazing lands around Collins Street in those days and, in spite of solemn warnings from the Governor in faraway Sydney that they were trespassing on Crown land, other settlers quickly followed, overland from the north and across the Bass Strait from the south.

The Governor soon realised there was no point in going on calling them trespassers, and despatched some officials and soldiers down there to make whatever was going on proper and official like.

What with free settlers arriving there from the Old Dart, the area was soon sufficiently established to demand recognition as the separate State of Victoria, which it received in 1850.

Perhaps it is the long-smouldering memory that her early inhabitants were deemed common trespassers by the powers-that-were in Sydney that has caused Melbourne ever since to pride herself on her gentility, her propriety, her decorum, as compared with the brash hustling settlement around Sydney Cove.

In the year 1836, the first settlers landed on the shores of South Australia, which had the most respectable origins of all Australian states. It was neither a penal colony nor a squatters' takeover, but a settlement of free men who actually paid for their land; minimum price 12/- per acre.

"What sort of new chums are we getting here now!" must have been the sardonic reflection of many of the old hands.

The simon-pure legality of this new breed, however, was soon sullied by numbers of emancipist overlanders who came in by the back door, so to speak, from New South to see what was going on.

There were much fewer Irish in South Australia than elsewhere, the virtues of sobriety and collars-and-ties were more highly regarded, and even today Adelaide still seems to have much longer Sundays than the other capital cities. Its hotels carry that aura of sorrowful gloom that characterises the drinking habits of all puritanical countries.

It is here, by an ironical twist of fate or agronomy, that most of the wines of Australia are produced.

The modern face of Australia was slowly taking shape. In the beginning there was only New South Wales, to be followed shortly by Van Diemen's Land, where a convict colony had been established in 1804.

Now, with the establishment of Victoria and South Australia, there were only two to go.

A penal settlement had been established at the mouth of the Brisbane River in 1824. But it was not until the pioneering overlanders, pushing their luck northwards from the Sydney area, came upon the fertile pastures of the Darling Downs, that things really got under way up there.

Again, as with Victoria, once there were sufficient numbers of them established in the district they got to thinking that they could govern themselves far better than some bloke in Sydney who knew nothing about it.

The state of the roads and sewerage systems in present-day Queensland has led some to believe that they were possibly mistaken. Nevertheless, in 1859 the State of Queensland was duly recognised.

Over in the west things moved more slowly. There had been some early fears that the French might poke their noses in, so to speak, and a party of some forty-four soldiers and convicts had been sent around there to raise the flag in 1826.

This they did at Albany, and three years later the main settlement was established at a place called Perth, which is still there.

The land in those parts, however, seemed to be composed largely of sand. An attempt at free settlement, backed by English capital, met with little success. Some camels were later imported, but they only served to discover how extensive the areas of sand really were, and there was no future in camel-farming as such.

Whereas those on the eastern seaboard of Australia felt themselves cut off from Europe, those in the west felt themselves cut off even from those in the east.

In 1850, when the east had stopped taking convicts, the west began importing them to cope with labour shortages; and it was not until 1890 that Western Australia was granted responsible colonial government.

Thus, the stage was set for the formation of modern Australia.

There were still a lot of blank spaces left, and indeed there still are, for people who wanted to get away from neighbours, but as far as the map went, the whole continent now fell within government boundaries of one kind or another.

The historical pattern of development had been one of men questing into the back blocks, and the government keeping tabs on them and telling them they were still governed when they got there.

The man in the bush resented this. He had scant respect for the man who did not know what the bush was like, and a widespread dislike and distrust of authority persists in Australian cities today, even though most of the men living there do not know what the bush is like and have no intention of finding out.

In a place so far from home, of homogeneous stock, all speaking the same language, there seemed no point in carrying on with six different governments all going their own way.

This was dramatically illustrated when Victoria built her railways with a five feet three inches gauge and New South Wales built hers with a four feet eight-and-a-half inches gauge, so that passengers from Sydney to Melbourne found themselves shuffling out of one train and on to another in the middle of the night in what should have been a straight-through journey.

In 1901 the federation of the six states was proclaimed and the Commonwealth of Australia was born.

The phobia of being governed by somebody sitting on his backside hundreds of miles away, which runs so strongly throughout the history of Australian settlement and was the main impulse behind the establishment of the states of Victoria and Queensland, was to reach its apotheosis in the establishment of Canberra as the federal capital; a place far enough from anywhere, and, according to an unnamed stockman on the Birdsville Track, "the biggest collection of backside-sitters of all time."

In general, one may say the history of Australia is more of a non-history.

No battles were fought on her soil; no dynasties rose and fell. Nobody ever got burnt at the stake or sent to the salt mines for holding the wrong ideas. There were no idling classes from which diplomats, generals, and the like have usually been drawn, and the outback was always a place more for dust and flies than pomp and pageantry.

The history books tell of the conflicts between man and man rather than between man and nature, and the early Australians were too busy in the struggle of making a living to make much in the way of history.

History was something that happened on the other side

of the world; to which Australia despatched expeditionary forces when the Old Country made the call.

It was not until the 1940s, when it was forcibly demonstrated that Britannia no longer ruled the waves, that the chill realisation struck home that history was something that could happen right down here in the South Pacific. The umbilical cord was severed, and, one way and another, Australia has been wondering what to do about it ever since.

2

THE POLITICAL LINE-UP

The ablest, the most energetic and the most public-minded citizens of any community are inevitably drawn into politics.

RETIRED CABINET MINISTER;
Surfers Paradise

I reckon politicians ought to work as well.

TIMBER GETTER;
Burramurra

Australia does not have the government it deserves. No politician could be that bad.

REFUGEE INTELLECTUAL;
Earls Court, London

Politicians? They're gas, man.

KINGS CROSS HIPPIE

In Australia there is no freedom to vote; only freedom on how to vote. You have to vote, whether you want to or not, and are fined for not doing so.

This makes for a higher turn-out of voters on election days than anywhere else in the world, except those countries where you can be shot for not doing so.

It does not, however, indicate a correspondingly high level of political awareness. It merely indicates a strong Australian antipathy towards paying fines, particularly when they can be avoided.

If you think that all politicians are useless, you can register a non-committal vote, but the size of this vote is never known.

If the votes of all candidates in one particular constituency are added together and then subtracted from the total number of votes available in that constituency, then the number of votes not given to any of the candidates can be calculated. But the breakdown of this vote, or rather non-vote, as it may be termed, into those who were too dense or too drunk to understand the ballot forms and those who were registering a sophisticated protest against politicians as such is never revealed.

Yet the feeling that all politicians are no good is possibly a majority sentiment among Australian voters; not only among the voters indeed, but even among the politicians themselves. The one unanswerable insult that can be thrown across the parliamentary benches in debate is to accuse an opponent of "making politics" of an issue.

If this sentiment were capably organised, it could well result in a sweeping triumph for the non-committal vote, which in effect would mean a House of Representatives with nobody sitting in it, an eventuality that is not provided for in the constitution. (See *The Possible Evolution of the Australian Political Situation.* Professor A. K. Grott, Head of Political Analysis, University of Australasia.)

But then, the organising of such a vote would call for another political party — an anti-political-party party, which would defeat its purpose by the fact of its own existence. (See Professor Grott's later work *Constitutional Anarchy — Why It Can Never Happen.*)

The siting of Canberra, far from every other Australian community of any size, is symptomatic of this national antipathy towards politicians; a feeling embedded deep in the Australian unconscious that, if there has to be a government, then let it be somewhere out of the way.

Once it was established there, of course, there developed the added resentment that the country is being run by a mob of politicians out in the scrub, who do not know what is going on half the time.

But the politicians do have to put their jobs up at election times and do have to maintain contact with their electorates. In fact, it is often held that they spend so much of their time travelling to and from Canberra and week-ending at home that they have no time left to govern the country properly, even if they had the brains to do so.

This feeds the suspicion that the country is really run by the men behind the scenes, those top-ranking Public Servants permanently domiciled in Canberra: blokes who never leave the place at all, immovable by popular vote, there for keeps, cut off from the rest of the country where the real work is done and going around in a sort of triplicated hothouse bureaucrat-in-wonderland atmosphere, thinking up yet more forms and permits to trip up the honest tax-payer, drawing fancy salaries and dreamtime pensions, and fixing themselves up the while with the best transport, sewerage and reticulated water supply systems in Australia. "No potholes in the roads up there, mate. They see to that—with our flamin' money."

Most political concern in Australia is on the parish-pump, or realistic level: when are they going to do something about the drains? rather than, where is democracy going?

In older, more closely-settled countries they have had that much longer to work on drainpipes and kerbs and channelling and service facilities generally. Things like being on the bitumen, and having water piped to the house, are taken for granted.

It is one of the unavoidable facts of town planning that when people are living closer together, a few miles of cable or underground piping serves the needs of more people than when they are living farther apart. In a scattered country like Australia, cautious officials in charge of the public purse-strings are constantly doubting the justification of laying twenty miles of gas mains or something when only a dozen ratepayers are going to be paying for it; a point of view that is liable to undermine what little confidence these ratepayers might have had in government in the first place.

To service the far-flung distances of Australia with anything like the standard of public highways found in a modern crowded European country would involve most of the populace in working for the Main Roads Department.

To a European eye, used to towering apartment blocks and nineteenth-century terrace houses, much of Australia has the aspect of a half-developed suburb where the workmen have not finished yet.

Now most sophisticated political debate is carried on in environments where all the mod. cons. of comfortable living are taken for granted. A man whose domestic water supplies depend on a rainwater tank is likely, should that tank be running dry, to be more worried about when it is going to rain again rather than what China is up to, or his government's attitude towards the latest regime in Venezuela.

So the general political temper, if there is such a thing, is ironic, unimaginative, down-to-earth, burgeoning with distrust; the approach essentially pragmatic.

Though the Labor Party has been strongly entrenched here since the turn of the century, there has been little impassioned dialectic on the rights and wrongs of who should own the means of production.

If a man fancies working for the State rather than a private boss, then the thing to do is get himself a job with the Post Office or the Railways or some other government department. The grand thesis that, since men work best when working for themselves, if the means of production are nationalised everybody would be working for himself by working for the State, because the State is what the people elect, never carried much weight here. It went against the deep-seated Australian conviction that in any set-up there are always a few bastards at the top giving out orders, and they can call themselves capitalists, commissars or anything else; and down below are the rest, doing the work and getting less pay for it. Bosses, like bushfires, are one of the unavoidable and unpleasant facts of life.

The disillusionment of Socialist theorising in the United Kingdom when it was discovered that a worker could be just as resentful about his job whether working for the National Millions Board or the Marquis of Grab; the fact that Russia now appears to be letting in a bit of private enterprise; that America has long since accepted the necessity of planning over a wide sector; and that generally such doctrinaire theorising one way or the other is now old hat, would seem to indicate that the rest of the world is beginning to catch up with the untutored Australian pragmatist, who knew from the start that all chiefs and no Indians was never on the cards anyway.

Intellectuals, as a class, have always been something of a back number in Australia. Indeed, an Australian intellectual is generally held to be something of a contradiction in terms, like a sunburnt Englishman or a phlegmatic Italian or a fun-loving Russian.

Outside the universities there is very little employment available for Australian intellectuals, and no *rentier* class to nurture them. There is not much demand for cosy literary weekend reviews. Three-quarters of the television channels are commercial, and the only possible use they could have for intellectuals would be as cleaners or night-watchmen at the studios. The Australian Broadcasting Commission gets most of its programmes of intellectual content from the British Broadcasting Corporation. An Australian caught reading a book when his lawn needs trimming or his car needs a greasing is reckoned to be on the slide to being a no-hoper.

True, there are statistics to show that the rate of book-buying per head in Australia is one of the highest in the world; but it is one of those statistics that has always baffled what few intellectuals there are, and is probably something to do with the fact that Australian parents have to buy textbooks for their children in State schools.

INTELLECTUS
AUSTRALIS
DO NOT FEED!

With the growth of the universities, however, things are changing somewhat.

Even in Queensland, traditionally regarded as the most frontier-like of all Australian states, where the only intellectuals around are stuffed and in museums, there has been a mass student protest march, roughly mauled by the police, on the issue of the right to hold protest marches.

Perhaps if the issue had been about something less academic — say the state of sewerage in Brisbane — public sympathy might have been more easily aroused. But as it was, quite a large number of the populace seemed to be on the side of the police, a rather un-Australian state of affairs.

The student demonstrator, as such, touches no deep reservoir of popular appeal. As elsewhere, there is a strong underground impression of blokes with beards and weirdy girl-friends — like the suspicion that Negroes have too much sex and not enough soap and water.

As the more conservative observers are quick to point out, the number of students who march in the streets is only a small fraction of the overall student population; the rest are busily and earnestly working for their degrees and a passport to a safe steady well-salaried career in the Public Service or such. And as for the marchers themselves: well, they're young; it's a phase they're going through. Give them another ten years; lumbered with wife, kids and mortgage, torpid in front of the telly after the day's grind, the missus on to them to do something about the guttering or to tidy up the garden, and they will have forgotten their youthful conceit of righting the world.

Revolution, after all, is something that happens in other continents over the sea. The sunny thirst-making climate of Australia makes the tax on beer a more pressing matter than the finer points of ideology.

Democracy is only a little over one hundred years old in Australia.

Not that it is much older anywhere else, but in Australia there were no preceding centuries of feudal oppression requiring a revolution to even things up a bit.

The nearest Australian equivalent to a baron or a squire would be the squatter, and the nearest to a peasant would be the small farmer, or cocky. But a cocky would be more likely to reach for his shotgun than touch his forelock if the squatter came round telling him what to do.

For the first thirty years or more the place was run by the Governor with the absolute powers of a tribal chief, except that he was not one of the tribe, being an officer appointed in London.

When a legislative council was formed to advise him, it consisted of members appointed by himself, and he could take or leave their advice as he thought fit, which was no great step along the road to democracy.

Eventually this council was enlarged to include elected members, but only men of substance elected by men of substance. This Squatters' Council, so-called, was all for more self-government; not for the Australian populace as such but for the Squatters' Council.

In the 1850s, this closed rural society was blown apart at the seams by the discovery of gold.

There was a great rush from the grazing properties to the diggings in Victoria, and people flocked in by the boatload from overseas, looking for El Dorado. For a while gold surpassed wool as the country's main export. Various manufacturing industries followed, trading and professional classes grew rapidly in numbers, and there was a general leavening of society after which the squatters were never again the power in the land that they had been.

The powers-that-were in London accepted that they were not dealing with a sort of outsize squatters' parish any more, and by the end of the decade all the States, with the exception of Western Australia, which was still taking in convicts, had secured self-government and the popular vote.

Not that there were any political parties to vote for to begin with. Political parties, with their fixed principles and dogmas about what they stand for, only come about as a result of thinkers on these problems sitting down and working on the finer points of political dialectic; and such activity is not widespread on sheep runs and goldfields.

The early members of parliament voted as loners, not according to party directions. This made for more individualism in the goings-on of parliament, but also for more corruption and political horse-trading; "You build the railway out to my constituency if you want my vote," sort of thing.

As elsewhere, there had been grave misgivings among the more conservative well-off elements about the wisdom of giving the common people the vote; a fear that the country would go to the dogs completely. But to begin with, members of parliament were not paid anyway, which kept out the no-hopers. The floodgates of anarchy were not opened, and the early colonial governments in all States behaved with that sense of responsibility that has always characterised men of wealth and substance everywhere.

The one big argument that caused a general division was between free traders and protectionists. Of the two most populous States, Victoria adopted a protectionist policy and New South Wales a free trade one, and such is the murkiness of economics that it is not clear to this day which was doing the right thing, as both States expanded and prospered, more or less.

By the end of the century, with education for all and militant trade unions and politicians being paid, thus enabling men without other means to stand for election, the Labor Party had become a power on the political scene, strong enough to hold the balance between the Free Traders and Protectionists, who soon forgot what it was they had been arguing about before and joined up in a common front against Labor, forming the Liberal Party; and this Lib-Lab conflict has been the dominating pattern of confrontation ever since.

A later party formed to protect the interests of primary producers, the Country Party, has in effect always lined up with the Liberal Party to keep Labor out of office; and the Labor Party has helped to keep itself out of office by an internal split which brought about the Democratic Labor Party, a splinter group, predominantly Roman Catholic, and much more zealous on anti-communism than the parent body.

But in a country where anti-boss sentiment is so strong, and where there are far more workers than bosses, it remains a mystery why the Labor Party has found itself out of office far more than it has been in; at least on the Federal level.

The folly of ever giving women the vote has been hinted at in some quarters as the reason for this.

The self-made man of business has nothing like the shining-example-of-what-can-be-done aura that he carries in the U.S.A.

Success in most fields, except sport, is automatically suspect. It is not absolutely certain that a man who has made a million is a ruthless scheming two-timing con man, but that is the way to lay the odds unless there are strong indications to the contrary. Honest work does not pay rates like that.

But communists, also, are men not to be trusted. They are generally thought of as stooges of Moscow or Peking, who should clear out and go there if they don't like it here.

In fact, distrust oozes pretty well all the way around. The primary producers look on the cities as full of men working part-time hours and not paying enough for their food. The townsfolk regard the farmers as a canny lot, always pleading poverty even when they are carting money to the bank. The workers know you can expect nothing in the way of honest dealing from the bosses, and the bosses hold much the same opinion about the unions. And, of course, everybody suspects the politicians.

In the absence of any strong doctrinaire ideology, which would only raise a horse laugh anyway, the essence of politics as the conflict and compromises of self-interested factions comes over strongly, and pressure groups abound on all sides.

The general atmosphere is one of wariness, apathy and cynicism, laced with the conviction that when you look around the world it is just about the best system there is.

In Europe, most of them live on house-blocks there would

not be room to build a decent garage on, and the workers and bosses are so far apart they do not even look and talk alike. America is one big rat-race chasing the almighty dollar, where they burn themselves out to get things they don't need to keep the advertisers going. And as for the rest, in those places where they have time to worry about anything else than where the next meal is coming from, they can get put away if they open their mouths in the wrong place at the wrong time.

"Flaming lucky we are down here, mate, when you come to reckon it all up," is the general consensus.

The most important pressure groups are the States themselves. Each State carried on with its own parliament after federation, making for a sort of split-level system of government. The State parliaments look after matters like roadways, drains, education, hospitals, law and order and, in fact, most aspects of government except national defence and foreign affairs.

The Labor Party has been much more successful in winning office on the State level than it has on the federal, which would seem to indicate something politically significant if one could only fathom out what it is.

It can hardly be that the populace feels that matters of national defence are safer in the hands of the Liberal Party, as in actual wartime it has usually been the Labor Party that has been elected to office.

Again, the protection of national economic interests provides no motive for distrusting the Labor movement, which has never been bogged down in any high-falutin' ideology like "Workers of the world unite."

There has always been a close tie-up between the trade unions and the Labor Party, and the White Australia policy had its grass roots in the protection of workers' interests, in which the main consideration was not: "Would you like your daughter to marry a coloured?" but rather: "Would you like your pay packet to look like a coolie's?"

Taxation is levied on a federal basis and each year the government has to decide how much to allocate out of the national purse to each state for its own development, which inevitably leads to an almighty financial haggle followed by outraged cries of "fair go" from six different quarters.

There are only two ways to resolve this annual argy-bargy. One is to scrap the state boundaries and run the whole country as one show. Regional culture as such is non-existent anyway, and there are no singularities of accent, outlook, manners or anything else to differentiate, say, a Queenslander from a Victorian, a Westralian from a Tasmanian. The Queenslander, Victorian, Westralian and Tasmanian have yet to be convinced of this, however; and any move to give the Canberra mob more powers than they have already meets with instant opposition, nudging that old Australian regret that there has to be any sort of government with any powers at all.

The other solution is to scrap federation and go back to having six different governments all going their own way; but in an age of satellites and electronic computers this is seen by the more shrewd political observers as a retrograde step towards the horse-and-buggy era, and not technologically viable.

Thus, the present cagey relationship between the States and Canberra is likely to continue into the foreseeable future, fortified with the traditional Australian trappings of mutual distrust and periodic rumblings of discontent about the way things are.

These rumblings tend to be more prevalent in Western Australia, which is the farthest away from Canberra and therefore the most suspicious of the federation set-up; and now that various mineral finds there have greatly strengthened the State's economy, there has been some talk of breaking away and hoisting the Westralian flag of independence, somewhere inland from Port Hedland.

Similarly, in the far north-east, where Russian, Chinese, and Japanese fishing boats are sighted offshore from time to time, helping themselves to Australian fish, and the Federal government has done nothing about it, there has been some demand, centred mainly in various bars around Cape York and the Gulf of Carpentaria, for a sovereign state of North Queensland, with its own navy to ensure that Australian fish find their way on to the Australian market to keep Australian fishermen going, regardless of what international law, whatever that is, might have to say about it.

This vague talk of secession, however, is not taken seriously, except possibly in Canberra itself, where it is rumoured that a group of highly-placed officials spend their time in research into the problems attendant upon such an eventuality.

The present political line-up, then, is likely to continue to the end of the century, and possibly to the end of the century after that, with "The preservation and improvement of Australian living standards, the maintaining of our traditional ties of kinship and mutual regard with the United Kingdom, the developing of ever-closer co-operation with our great and powerful ally the United States of America, and the fostering of friendship and goodwill and the promotion of economic and cultural relationships with all our Asian neighbours," as the avowed policy of whichever party is in office, and also of the party in opposition.

3

THE ECONOMIC MIX-UP

The problems of harnessing Australia's natural resources to the maximum benefit of the whole community must never be divorced from a consideration of what those resources really are.

AN ANALYSIS OF CERTAIN ASPECTS OF THE
AUSTRALIAN ECONOMIC PREDICAMENT.
D. O. GRUMPEN,
Faculty of Economic Semantics, U. of Aust.

If Australia continues to pay her way she will not go bankrupt.
THE PRIME MINISTER

When Australia was first set up as a penal colony, the authorities in London decided that there was no need for money out there. After all, convicts were not paid wages; the settlement, it was hoped, would soon be self-supporting, and some simple system of barter would be adequate to keep the economy going.

The officers of the garrison, in fact, were virtually the only people with money to spend, and these gentlemen soon formed a monopoly over all the rum that came into the colony, as it was discovered that the promise of drink was the best way to get the felons to do any work.

Thus, the New South Wales Corps, the quasi-military force raised in England to garrison the colony, acquired its notorious sobriquet of "The Rum Corps," and rum became the vital currency that appeared to keep the wheels turning for a while.

It is held by some that this is still the broad economic picture, except that beer has been substituted for rum and the workers now get paid in money which they then convert to liquor, as the owners of the liquor are no longer the employers of labour, thus creating a class of entrepreneurs known as publicans.

In an age of oil mergers, preferential share issues, debenture stock holdings and the rest, this is something of an over-simplification. In fact, considering the size of its population, Australia now has as many pundits on economic affairs as any other sophisticated industrialised country; experts who speak in a manner largely unintelligible to the community at large, laying a verbal smokescreen of specialised terminology through which it is difficult to discern whether they are talking sense or nonsense.

Yet the fundamental economic picture of Australia as a populated coastal fringe around an enormous empty and largely useless interior has not changed all that much since the beginning; just that there has been a phenomenal increase in the number of experts depicting the way things are.

In Australia, unlike America, the pioneering trails and ensuing settlement petered out a few hundred miles from the coast.

This was not because the American pioneers had more guts or staying power—he would indeed be a foolhardy man who ventured such an opinion in any bar from Gundagai to Tennant Creek—but rather because when you went a certain distance inland from the Australian coast it stopped raining, sometimes for years on end, and the only thing that would grow was spinifex, and ants and lizards were the only creatures that could get by.

This in itself was no bad thing. After all, the quality of life does not reside in mere quantity, and the fact that there are so many more people living in places like Chicago and St Louis does not mean that they are necessarily better places in which to live than Darwin or Alice Springs. It might be just that there are more people unable to get away from them because of various commitments.

In fact, it is held by some that it is a good thing to have a few large areas of the earth's surface left largely uninhabited by humans, so that those oddballs who want to get away from their fellow men can do so.

Dr Reginald Poundfellow, Reader in Social Psychiatry, U. of A., in his book *The Masses And What Keeps Them At It*, claims that no less than 69.7 per cent of the wage-earners of the vast unending suburbs of Sydney and Melbourne are kept going through their daily routines of factories and offices and peak-hour traffic snarls by the fantasy that one day they are going to throw it all in and shoot through for the Birdsville Track and beyond. And though these fantasies are rarely, if ever, acted out, the fact that they exist is of enormous therapeutic value.

The blank interior of Australia may thus be playing a significant role in the maintenance of sociological stability as a daydream safety valve for harassed city dwellers.

From the standpoint of economics, however, it is just a blank, and responsible for the "vacuum syndrome" that has dominated so much of Australian economic thinking; the feeling that so much blankness on a map means that things are not finished yet, that this is still an empty land that needs filling up.

There are two schools of thought on this issue, as indeed there must be for the creation of any issue; there are the visionaries and the snag-seers.

The snag-seers contend that there is no point in trying to make things grow up north, just because there is nobody there, when the same things can be grown more economically down south. Three-quarters of the Australian continent, they hold, is uninhabitable, and it becomes more so the farther you go from Sydney, Melbourne, Brisbane, Adelaide and Perth.

The visionaries, on the other hand, see the development of the interior as merely waiting upon the necessary but inevitable advances in technology, particularly since the main cause of non-development is lack of water, in a land which is set in one of the vastest expanses of water on the surface of the earth.

The most imaginative project to resolve this incongruity is that put forward by the Bureau for Economic Advancement and Big Thinking (B.E.A.B.T.), which envisages two gigantic irrigation channels across the continent, one running from north-west to south-east, and the other from north-east to south-west, bisecting somewhere about Tennant Creek, in the centre of the Dead Heart. At the four entrances to these two channels huge desalination plants will treat the ocean water for agricultural use, and innumerable smaller channels will lead off from the basic structure to serve those vast tracts of the interior which only get rain once or twice in a decade.

Any areas of land beyond the reach of this tremendous irrigation system will be peppered regularly with artificial rainclouds, thus completing the transformation of the desolate interior into the prairies of the South Pacific or some such vital role.

There are others who see the settlement of the interior in terms of a mining, rather than a farming community. The red desert plains, the barren hills and the creek beds are being combed for mineral deposits as never before; not by fossickers with picks and pans and swags and a half-crazy glint in the eye, but by young men with degrees in geology and four-wheel drive vehicles, employed by international mining corporations.

There are constant announcements of yet more discoveries of coal, copper, iron, nickel, uranium, bauxite, oil, and natural gas beneath the hard dry crust of the interior.

"We are not being unduly optimistic," a spokesman for one of these mining corporations said recently, "when we claim that we have already located sufficient uranium to blow Australia right out of the sea."

The more radical visionaries of this school see the economic destiny of Australia as a continental mining lease. They hold that it is wasteful and inefficient to try and raise any crops here at all. The land, by and large, is dry, dusty and barren, with the occasional devastating flood breaking the recurring droughts.

Not far away to the north are the fertile paddy fields of Asia. What is required, they maintain, is a radical re-orientation of Australian eating habits; away from steak, chops, sausages, and meat pies, to rice, noodles, and chicken chow mein.

Our enormous mineral wealth will supply the developing industries of Asia with the raw materials they will need so desperately; in exchange for which they will supply us with the foodstuffs we need to continue mining.

Such an economic integration of this area of the globe, which will follow upon Australia finally ridding herself of the fantasy that she is part of Europe, will eventually cause a mass movement of the bulk of the Australian population from the south-east corner of the continent to the north-west, where the most striking mineral finds have been made. Sydney and Melbourne will become ghost towns of an obsolescent and misguided past.

All this, however, is very much in the future.

To get back to the present, or rather the past, which is where the present begins.

The early simplicities of the Australian economy disappeared with the discovery of gold and the subsequent development of secondary industries.

Up till then it had been possible to regard the country productionwise as a very large sheep station. Men either grazed sheep or sheared sheep or carted wool along the bullocky trails or loaded wool on to the waiting ships. The only city of any size, Sydney, was more or less a gigantic warehouse and transport depot, with wool going through one way and tea, tobacco, flour and various other provisions for the sheep stations outback going through the other. The economy of the country as a whole prospered or faltered according to the size of the wool cheque, and there was no need for a Department of Economic Affairs staffed with university graduates regularly taking the nation's pulse as a going business concern.

The central dilemma of the Australian economy, however, was already in evidence; what the country produced was sold overseas, so the health of the nation's economy was thus tied up to the uncertainties of overseas markets.

Wool graziers have long since ceased to be the only primary producers to be found in Australia. There are now dairy farmers, fruit farmers, wheat farmers, and sugar cane farmers, all producing in excess of the demands of the home market, and thus causing the Australian government to shop around with shiploads of apples, grain, butter and sugar to see what they can get in exchange in the way of such things as swing-wing jet aeroplanes, radar tubes, electronic computers and transistor tape recorders.

These transactions are never carried out on a simple barter basis. International finance comes into it; which means in effect that the bloke growing grapes on the

Murray, apart from having to battle with drought, frost, flood and downy mildew, also has to worry about what bankers and financiers in places like New York, London, Geneva and Tokyo are up to.

Australia being where it is, the local dairy farmer trying to sell his butter in an overcrowded island like the United Kingdom is under a distinct handicap compared with his opposite number in, say, Denmark or Ireland; countries which also have a fair number of cockies trying to make out with a few milkers. The Australian cocky suffers from what economists would call "the market price differential resulting from variation of geographical proximity." Or, as a non-economist would say, the farther you are away from the market the more you've got to pay for cartage.

We would be better off, in fact, selling the butter in Asia if only they had the wherewithal to pay for it. Or in New Zealand if they had not got so much butter of their own that they don't know what to do with it.

Or again, if the price of butter on the home market was cut, this could lead to increased consumption. If Australian butter cost no more in Sydney or Melbourne than it does in London, then Australians would no doubt eat more of it. But it is held that there are not enough Australian consumers to justify this move.

It all gets very complicated. Should subsidies and protective tariffs be withdrawn? Should ploughs be left to rust and land be left to waste if the farmers cannot hold out on an open market? Dairy herds and fruit blocks are not things that can be switched back into production overnight, once they have been let go.

To understand the finer intricacies of the old Free Trade versus Protection argument, that has dominated the Australian economic scene from the beginning, one would have to spend a lifetime working at the Department of Economic Affairs, and it is by no means certain that those who have actually done so know what to do either.

The consumer wants to shop around and get the best value he can for his money, and the cheaper the goods are the better, whether made in Melbourne or Hong Kong.

On the other hand, the idea that the workers in Melbourne should start getting the sort of wages they get in Hong Kong is unthinkable. And the fact of the consumer and the wage-earner being by and large the same person makes it all the more complicated.

Should the market be flooded with cheap duty-free overseas goods that people cannot afford anyway, because they have been put out of work by them? Or should protective tariffs be high enough to ensure that people still cannot afford them, so that their non-sale will make the Australian workers' jobs safe?

These are the kind of questions that give senior officials of the Department of Trade in Canberra that look of haunted and irreplaceable gloom.

At the heart of the dilemma is the question of Australian wages, which, understandably, is the only interest that most Australians have in the subject of economics.

As is often pointed out in statistics on such matters, the great majority of Australians own houses, cars, fridges, tellys, and washing machines. What is not pointed out, however, is how many of them have actually paid for these things and how many are living on the never-never.

In no way has Australia become more thoroughly Americanised than in the style of "possess now, pay later." In fact, it is estimated that if all the motor cars not paid for were taken off the roads, the roads would become more or less safe for traffic.

The level of industrial wages is fixed by haggling between managements and unions and arbitration tribunals, which have the power to fine unions if they do not abide by their findings.

Increases are given on the basis that those who need them least get the most. Thus, a senior public official earning $15,000 a year will get a further two or three thousand to keep him in line with his counterparts in commerce, while a man struggling along on about forty-eight dollars a week might get another $1.35. These meagre calculated-to-the-cent increments for the masses are arrived at after solemn cogitation on all the factors involved by senior Government Commissioners, usually men of high legal standing and dictatorial powers and no experience of living near the knuckle, who may be earning anything up to $20,000 a year. The final mental exertions whereby a man earning $400 a week decides, after weighing up what the national economy can afford, that another earning fifty dollars a week is to have an increase of $1.35 or $1.40, are never revealed. But someone has to decide it, and for a country with the great levelling traditions of Australia, the system is accepted with surprisingly little demur.

The great whinge goes up when the politicians vote themselves an increase, and are seen to be earning huge salaries from the standpoint of most of the voters. Though, compared with senior business executive levels, their salaries are in fact quite modest.

There is a basic wage, laid down by law in all Australian states, which all employers must pay. It is so low by Australian standards, however, that any employer paying just that would find it difficult to attract labour, so it does not mean much.

What would be more to the point would be a maximum wage, beyond which no-one would be allowed to earn, as it is estimated that by the end of the century, if present trends continue, while the bulk of the populace will still be struggling in a morass of hire purchase payments, accountants, lawyers, doctors, university professors, senior Public Servants, business executives and other top echelons of managerial society will be earning so much money that they will be breaking down under the strain of trying to work out what to do with it all.

Meritocracy, in fact, like the aristocracies of old, rolls along on the old biblical principle of "to them that hath more shall be given."

The unions have largely lost what firebrand militancy they had in harder times. Meetings, except when there is a strike in the air, are largely unattended, except by a handful of officials and shop stewards. The rot of establishment has set in, creating that gap between leaders and rank-and-file, and the old traditional Australian habit of distrust has swamped in. The union leaders, ensconced in their Trades Hall strongholds, carry on lengthy involved arguments with employers' representatives about the finer points of arbitration techniques, but it arouses little interest or enthusiasm on the work benches.

Once a man is set up with an office and collar-and-tie and spends his days arguing the point he has stopped being a worker; he has become one of "them." "He's doing all right for himself, mate," is the feeling he leaves behind.

Dues are often paid with varying degrees of reluctance; union organisation is geared to chasing up subscriptions from unwilling members, even to the use of debt-collecting agencies and threats of legal action, and any increase in subscription dues serves to confirm the suspicion that "they know what they're doing all right; they're got it all fixed."

In some jobs where union membership is a condition of employment, the union dues are deducted on the payroll before the worker gets his pay packet, which only goes to strengthen the vague suspicion that there is some sort of tie-up between the union bosses and the straightforward bosses, both of whom are on the other side of the fence to the honest worker.

By and large, however, inequalities and hire purchase payments notwithstanding, working conditions and pay in Australia are on a different level from those obtaining among her Asian neighbours, where the masses are still bowed down under a feudal yoke.

And this makes for all sorts of knotty problems, particularly now that trading links with Asia need to be developed while those with the United Kingdom, dithering on the brink of the Common Market, fade away.

There is the phenomenal rise of Japan as one of the industrial giants of the world, where it seems that a kind of feudal paternalism has been carried over into a mass production society.

There workers seem to settle for a life-time contract of employment with one firm. They do not jack in their jobs and shoot through like they do in Australia. They do not take days off to back horses or go on the beer. They expect less in the way of wages and smoke-oh breaks, and toil away on the production lines with a termite-like tenacity.

A society in which work is regarded as the reason for living is obviously going to turn out cheaper goods than one where work is regarded as a regrettable necessity, getting in the way of more civilised pursuits like fishing and drinking and going to the drive-in.

It had been thought, or perhaps hoped, by some people that Asians did not really understand engineering; that when their cars were put on the road the gearboxes would jam, or the crankshafts would not turn, or the wheels would fall off; but this generally has not been the case.

Japanese cars, by and large, work as well as Australian, British and American cars, and, unless stopped by tariffs, turn out to be somewhat cheaper.

The Australian public is all for having cheap cars, the cheaper the better as long as they go all right, but, quite understandably, is all against anything like Asian working conditions being introduced into Australia.

"Do you want a car manufacturing industry here?" demand the car manufacturers.

"Certainly we do," replies the government. "A car manufacturing industry is a vital element in a sophisticated industrialised economy."

"Then you have got to protect us against unfair competition," say the manufacturers.

But then it is reasonable to suppose that if Japanese

imports to Australia are to be subject to high tariffs, then Australian exports to Japan will be subject to the same.

Words like technology, computers, and automation are bandied about when the threat of cheap mass labour elsewhere comes under discussion. But in an age when the Chinese are supposed to be getting on with the H-bomb out in the Gobi Desert, the technological gap between East and West takes on a rapidly dwindling significance. The uneasy feeling persists that the writing is on the wall; that things will only be sorted out eventually by Japanese workers taking more smoke-ohs, or Australian workers taking less.

An intensive education programme, aimed at the toiling masses of Asia, has been suggested as a means of alleviating this threat to the Australian economy. They must be made to realise that there is more to life than increasing factory output; that work is not an end in itself but something that gets in the way of living, and this is something that workers everywhere must realise, because, if one lot of workers persists in working unremittingly for little reward, they can, through repercussions on the world markets, put the knockers on it for the others.

Information centres could be set up in the main Asian cities, with free film shows showing the Australian worker on the beach, in the bar, at the stadium. Scenes of Australian life at places like Randwick and Caulfield, at the stock car meetings and the drive-ins, could be given a wide circulation, with the constant exhortation that this could be the life for workers everywhere.

Broadcasting could play an important role, with daily programmes in various Asian languages emphasising the desirability of a leisured and adequately-paid society, and relating the Australian concept of "fair go" to international economics—if we have to compete on the world markets then let us do it under the same handicaps of a forty-hour working week, regular smoke-ohs and holidays.

An interesting proposal put forward by the Brewers' Association is for government subsidy of a huge export programme of Australian beer to Asian markets at rock bottom prices. If Asian workers can be encouraged to drink beer to the same extent as Australian workers, it is held, then the competition of Asian manufactured commodities will be that much easier to deal with, and if it is Australian beer that they are drinking then so much the better for our balance-of-payments problems *vis-a-vis* Asia.

Beer drinking, however, has never had the appeal in Asia that it has had for westerners. The Japanese, and it is they who come foremost to mind when thinking of the economic threat of Asia, seem to prefer a weird drink called *saké*, and, so far from it lowering their working potential to any noticeable degree, there is no reason to suppose they would

drink great quantities of Australian beer even if it were given away.

Anyway, competition rather than co-operation has always been the prevailing spirit, indeed the essence, of international business affairs, and the economic predicament of Australia as an urbanised westernised technological managerial consumer-orientated offshore continent with a high living standard, geographically isolated from similar societies and offshore to a larger, hitherto backward but rapidly changing ideology-riven continent with a low living standard, is, one may say with some degree of prophetic certainty, fraught with uncertainty.

The traditional trade links with the United Kingdom are dwindling away. What new links are to be forged in their place? In the contemporary complex world situation of revolutionary change, trade links with anybody can mean trouble, uncertainty, crisis. So the fundamental question must be posed — do we, in fact, need trade links at all?

Possibly because of the origin of the country as a far-flung colony at the end of shipping lanes, an outpost of an older established civilisation, there has always been an underlying assumption that overseas trade was a vital part of the Australian economy, as indeed it was when wool was more or less the only product, apart from mutton. There are decided limits to the extent that an economy producing only wool can carry on trade within itself. But in the last 120 years, particularly in the last twenty, there has been some diversification of the economy. The merino ram no longer dominates the country's output potential, and it is time to recognise this factor.

True, if imports were to cease completely, such luxuries as venison, caviare, Scotch grouse and coconuts would be unobtainable. But would it matter? Would the bulk of the populace even notice?

Traditionally Asian commodities, such as rice, cotton and tea, are now grown on Australian soil. We are now finding our own oil, have long had our own coal, and the production lines of Australian factories can turn out pretty well everything needed in the way of manufactured commodities. What, in fact, do we need from overseas that cannot be produced here?

If a country has to import, then it seems it has to export as well, and if the value of the exports do not come up to the value of the imports then it has something called a balance-of-payments crisis; it is in economic trouble.

Conversely, there is no need for exports unless one has to pay for imports. Indeed, if such imports would be a threat to home production, it might be more sensible not to make the exports that make such imports possible.

Consider the millions of tons of iron ore and coal now contracted to be shipped to Japan over the remainder of the century. If these minerals are going to return in the form of motor cars and what not to knock out the Australian car manufacturing industry, among other things, then it might be wiser to leave them where they are underneath the bush until such times as they can be used in Australia. Possibly a giant industrial plant could be built somewhere in the Northern Territory, which would be the most favourable location to utilise both the iron ore of Western Australia and the coal of central Queensland in the one process.

Could it be that by the twenty-first century Western Australia and Queensland will be denuded of mineral wealth, liable to chronic subsidence because all the rocks have been honeycombed, and with nothing to show for it except large holes in the ground, several lengths of disused railway track connecting ghost mining towns with crumbling harbour facilities, and a load of Japanese yen in the bank, the value of which could be sent crashing overnight by the jiggery-pokery of bankers and speculators in places like Tokyo, New York and Zurich?

A million tons of ore mined, refined and marketed is an asset gone for ever, like an extracted tooth, but a million dollars or a million yen in the bank is a few figures on a piece of paper, and anything can happen in those shadowy processes where wealth is converted into money.

A country not dependent on imports, and consequently under no necessity to export, can stand aside from the lunacies of international finance; the runs on dollar and sterling, the uncertainties of the yen and the franc, the recurring monetary crises and the backstairs machinations of anonymous bankers and speculators in far away cities.

Has Australia, in fact, reached this state without realising it? Has there been some fatal breakdown of communication of the economy to itself, as it were, so that, in mining, for example, though having the machinery, the labour and the know-how, it is held not to be possible to begin extracting the vast mineral deposits that are there until various figures and signatures go on to bits of paper in banks and offices in

London or New York, authorised by financiers who know nothing about mining and who possibly have never been to Australia?

A country, after all, need not be hamstrung by lack of money in the way that an individual may be. A country, unlike an individual, prints its own, and it is quite legal for it to print more if it finds itself a bit short. In fact, it may be held that a function of a nation's treasury is to see that there is enough paper currency going around to ensure that full use can be made of the country's real wealth, which, of course, is not money at all but soil, oil, coal, gas, iron ore and the like.

Any loans necessary for development can then be made from the government, and the interest derived therefrom can go into social amenities and not into financiers' pockets.

But so far from making loans to get things going, the Australian government seems to be flat out trying to raise loans itself from overseas. In fact, the wealthier the country finds itself, the more it seems to need to borrow money, which would seem to indicate a definite departure, somewhere along the line, from common sense.

Government, right down to city level, seems to be caught in this dilemma of overseas borrowing. The Brisbane City Council, for example, recently financed extensions to its sewerage system by a loan of several million dollars, at appropriate rates of interest, from European financiers. To quote from Professor Grumpen before he was remanded for psychiatric observation: "Borrowing money in Europe to enable Australian trench-digging machinery manned by Australian labour to commence digging Australian sewerage trenches is usury gone mad."

Will the nation wake up one morning and find itself mortgaged to the hilt? Will the government then shut shop and the financiers take over? Will they be empowered to sell the country off, and, if so, to whom?

Nation-wise, in fact, the economy seems to be in the throes of some pretty weird book-keeping. At what point does common sense get lost in the maze of economic practice? It is a matter for the experts to unravel.

Or is it, perhaps, because of the experts that things are as they are?

If Australia were to cut adrift from the imbroglio of economic conventions; if it were to take the attitude of a country that can feed itself, manufacture for itself, print money for itself adequate to its own requirements without the need for overseas borrowing, and generally look after itself irrespective of the canons of international finance, then there would be no need for an army of experts analysing the money markets of the world and making predictions about inflation, deflation, import quotas, dollar deficiencies, credit restrictions and the rest of it. Horse sense would replace expertise and a lot of economists would be out of a job.

It is unlikely, therefore, that advice to move in this direction will come from the usual advice-giving quarters, as the profession that advocates its own demise has yet to be found.

4

THE SOCIAL SET-UP

In Australian society the men and the women play two different roles.

Aspects of Pacific Anthropology,
Professor K. D. Plunkett.

The first authentic picture we have of Australian society is found in the journals of that charming Victorian gentleman-traveller-dilettante, Gilbert Fish, who wrote: "In social gatherings, I noticed, the men and women kept very much to themselves, and never did I get the impression on my travels around that continent that it was generally thought to be the happiest arrangement of nature that compelled men and women to cohabit at all.

"The men tend to be spare of build, to walk and talk with the barest economy of movement and expression, to be bothered very little about dress, and never seem so happy as when going off to do some fishing and leaving the women-folk behind. The women, far from resenting this, seem pleased to have the menfolk out of the way for a while. In fact, I would say that for the natives of Australia social and sexual intercourse do not have the happily complementary disposition that is such a desirable element for a harmonious society within the canons of western culture. Perhaps the location in the Pacific has some relevance here."

Unfortunately, it is not clear from the context whether the writer is referring to the Aborigines or, as it were, us.

There is no such ambiguity in a slightly later writer, Sir Giles Ponsonby-Pemberton, who wrote: "In the better houses I was entertained in as good a style as you could expect in the colonies. Everybody was very proper in their dress and behaviour, the fact of my being a baronet occasioned a proper amount of respect, not a few confided in me that they sadly missed the gentler airs and manners of "home," and in these circles, at any rate, everybody looked to England as setting the standards that were to be followed.

"Among the common people outside, however, this was not at all the case. I had occasion to rebuke one fellow in the street one day for some minor impertinence, and demanded of him, "Do you know who I am?"

"A flaming pom by the sound of it," he replied. "And if you don't like it here why don't you clear off back to where you came from?"

"This, I was told later by my hostess, was typical of the lower orders here; no respect for their betters, caring nothing for English standards, but Australian, if you please, and very pleased about it; not at all apologetic, rather the reverse, for the manner in which they or their forebears came out here, and generally carrying on as though the country belonged to them."

No date can be set for when the majority of the population started regarding themselves as Australians rather than displaced Englishmen, though it is safe to assume it happened much more quickly among the emancipists than among those who came out here of their own free choice, as one would naturally tend to feel less association with a place one had been turfed out of.

Then the large Irish element seem to have experienced little difficulty with being displaced Irishmen. Their animus was mainly directed to being anti-English rather than ex-

Irish, which was something more easily incorporated into an Australian identity.

Society here never had the clean democratic start that American society had. From the beginning there was the division between the bond and the free, though that social schism has long disappeared into the dustbin of time.

To be able to trace your forbears to the First Fleet now has something of the social cachet of tracing them back to the Norman Conquest in England. You were one of the first here; how you came to be here is no longer important at this point in time.

Though the land was there for the taking in the early days, there was no point in taking it unless you had the capital to stock a run. The squatters, therefore, tended to be free settlers with a bit of money behind them; possibly officers of the New South Wales Corps, men on the make, who intended retiring to the comfortable green shires of England when they had made it.

The ex-convicts, the ticket-of-leave men and their descendants, here for keeps and no bones about it, were more likely to be found working as bullockies or among the itinerant bands of shearers and drovers and casual labourers.

Far from the cosy tea-and-muffins social niceties of old England they might be, but the squatters saw themselves as a class apart from this mob; and even to this day there are tales of graziers out on the lonely western plains dressing for dinner, and generally upholding the burdens of the English landed gentry in a rough colonial land.

The far-flung grander homesteads of the outback are, in fact, one of the last reserves of that genteel relic of a vanished age — the nanny, or children's governess, giving the children the rudiments of learning before they are packed off to boarding school.

Women, or rather the lack of them, and the enormous distances and isolation have given the outback its own distinctive form of society; harsh, boozy, hierarchical.

There are the boss and his missus in the homestead, their social relationships confined to other bosses and their missuses in scattered homesteads over the neighbouring few hundred square miles. The men live in their quarters, drifting, womanless, rolling their own smokes and going into town for a periodic binge; the hard cases who have given society away.

This is the Australia they know about overseas and most Australians only know about through seeing it on the movies; the land of the stock whip and the water hole, the flying doctor and the pedal wireless, the man in the broad-brimmed hat out on his own in a hard pitiless land with the odds stacked against him.

The subtle social nuances of this lonely world are well caught in that as yet unperformed Australian opera, *Bluey*, in which Imogen, the wealthy grazier's daughter, falls in love with Bluey, a handsome itinerant union organiser of the shearing sheds. Her father, shocked to hear of his daughter's choice, instantly flies off to Sydney in his private plane, returning with a first class world cruise ticket, which he throws on the table in front of his daughter. In a moving scene Imogen tells her father that she would sooner live with Bluey in Booroolugillah than see Rome, Paris, London, New York, Honolulu and Suva, and tears up the ticket in front of him.

Realising the depth of his daughter's passion, the father decides to make the best of it and takes Bluey into the homestead as a jackeroo. But when there is a spot of trouble with the men in the sheds and Bluey goes to sort it out, he hears muttered remarks on all sides of "Boss's man"; "Woman's man"; "Ratbag". Realising that he has lost the regard of his mates for the sake of a sheila, and knowing at the same time that he cannot live without Imogen, Bluey wanders off into the bush singing a moving aria to the effect that you can't win in this world, a true-blue Aussie sentiment.

Outside the half-dozen capital cities on the coast, there are only a dozen or so towns of any size at all; towns in which a man could live a lifetime and not know who everybody was.

For the rest, the endless waiting sun-scarred distances are dotted with small dusty townships with a straggle of stores and service stations along the one main drag, and accommodating perhaps a schoolie, a bankie, a bookie, a copper and a few other pillars of the community.

The main feature of these places is their lack of features, their lack of regionalism, their similarity. Despite the enormous distances, the variations of climate and landscape, there are none of the differences of accent, custom, locality that exist between, say, Cornwall and East Anglia or Northumberland and Sussex in the United Kingdom.

A small town in the cane-growing north of Queensland is farther from a town in the mallee scrub of Victoria than London is from Madrid. But about the only difference between the Queenslander and the Victorian would be that one was worried about the price of sugar and the other about the price of wheat.

There is no solid provincial society such as you find in older, more closely-settled countries. No Madame Bovary waits, in places like Cunnamulla or Broken Hill, for some Australian Flaubert to come along and record her languors and her dreams.

There is the bush, and the city.

Not that the bush is all big-time graziers living in colonial-baronial splendour in their far-flung homesteads. Nearer the coast, where rainfall permits, the land is closely cultivated, and the huge grazing properties give way to the selection blocks where the small farmer struggles to make a living by getting things to grow.

Between the struggling cockie and his few acres, and the established outback grazier, is the whole social ladder of rural society.

So far from dressing for dinner, the cockie is liable to go into town in his singlet if he is stuck for a roll of fencing wire or a bag of fertiliser.

The wealthy grazier may have his own light aeroplane as well as a late model station sedan and a smaller car for the missus. He pops up to Sydney or Melbourne for a week at showtime and for other social highlights of the year, leaving instructions to the hired hands about what to do on the property in his absence.

The cocky may run a rattling old ute with three bald tyres, and his social outings are limited to an occasional couple of schooners at the local bar. So far from paying wages to hired hands, he would go and work for wages himself and pay off his bank overdraft if he could find somebody mug enough to buy the place off him.

Inasmuch as there are more of him, he is more typical of the Australian man-on-the-land than the well-off grazier. A man of property he might be, but he is likely to be having a harder time, in the sense of working far longer hours with less to show for it in the bank, than most of the wage-earners in the comfortable city suburbs.

The corrugated lean-tos around the peeling makeshift homesteads of the struggling small farmer have an impermanent look about them; across much of the Australian rural landscape is the air of fighting a losing battle against the age-old and ever-encroaching bush.

It is in the cities that Australian society is most confidently established; where Western European suburbanite seems to have really licked his South Pacific environment into order.

The five mainland state capitals are a bit like the city states of ancient Greece; beleaguered concentrations of civilisation against a pretty blank background, with something of the same idolatry of sport but none of the penchant for philosophy.

Each has its stock image. Sydney; Americanised, raw and brash and hustling, with its Kings Cross reserve of seedy cosmopolitan glamour — whores, strippers, bohemians and bon vivants. Melbourne; Anglicised, decorous and proper, the city in the grey flannel suit, the centre of business and banking. Brisbane; the overgrown sun-blistered hick town, with the funny houses on stilts and the feel of the bush on the doorstep. Perth; quiet and easy and sunny, a good place for retirement. Adelaide; planned and purposeful and eminently respectable, a bit staid and churchy, in fact.

But beneath the hackneyed clichés lies the same tidy suburban pattern, of a practical outgoing race adapting to a sub-tropical environment.

The puttering of lawn mowers breaks the week-end quiet across the vast stretches of chamferboard and brick veneer and fibro; each house standing on its own block. There is so much room to spread outwards. Outside a few inner city areas, terraced housing is virtually non-existent.

The legions of homeowners, busy with hammer-and-nails and pots of paint, give the lie to the popular image of the Saturday Australian as supine on the beach or three parts gone at the bar or losing his shirt at the races.

Surprisingly large areas of these suburbs are without hotels at all. A lot of the drinking is done at home, with queues of cars forming at the drive-in-take-away bottle sale counters, and an easy informal come-around-to-my-place-I've-got-a-couple-in-the-fridge mode of hospitality. Those who pack the long sleazy comfortless bars tend to be sad men without wives, or sadder men with wives they want to get away from.

It is in these spreading city suburbs that the fabled Australian ideal of a mass leisured affluence in the sun comes closest to realisation; the garden sprinkler playing on the lawn, the telly flickering in the lounge, the car waiting in the garage to whisk the young to the surf breakers or the oldies to their bowling.

Australian cities are free of the urban tensions that now plague the American scene, possibly because there have never been enough coloured immigrants allowed in to discover the extent of racial prejudice which exists.

The general attitude towards the Aboriginal, at least in the cities, where he poses no threat to the stability of white society, is one of interest in his traditions and liberal concern for his welfare; but this gets markedly less so as one goes towards the north and the interior where most of the Aborigines are found; where the Abo and his lubra tend to become the boong and the gin, and where, with the scarcity of white womenfolk, sex has become a serious problem.

There has been a decided break-up of the old British homogeneity of stock with the post-war open immigration policy from Southern Europe, but these new elements have been absorbed with little friction. True, when an Aussie who has spent thirty years drinking beer and backing losers and has nothing to carry him through except next week's pay packet, looks around and sees a thrifty New Australian owning a nice farm or restaurant, he is not slow to draw the inference that this country will soon be owned by a pack of flaming foreigners. But these individual suspicions of foreign takeover have produced no serious rifts in the general process of assimilation.

As there are no class distinctions in the European sense, Australia is often spoken of as a classless society, which it is in the sense that there are no striking differences of accents, clothes or style. However, it is not so in the sense that some live in weatherboard shacks and fill up on potato and pumpkin and get cake on Sundays if they are lucky, while others live in grand mansions and get cake every day.

The social divisions are essentially a matter of money; not whether you eat your peas with a knife or sleep in your vest or can come out with the apt quotation in French or Latin, but whether you have a bank manager or not, and, if you have, the way he looks at you.

Instead of the working class, the middle class, and the aristocracy, there are those who are struggling, variously estimated at between 5 and 95 per cent of the population; those who are comfortable, not short of a dollar or two; and those who are rolling in it.

In a recent survey of the twelve wealthiest men in Australia, it was revealed that three thought Picasso was a French racehorse, two thought the Roman Empire included America, six thought Shakespeare was a nineteenth century writer and seven thought the Renaissance was something to do with the European Common Market, while all of them thought that anyone who did not want to work for a living should be shot.

There is thus no refined elegant upper class cultivating the arts of leisure, such as set the tone for society in eighteenth century England or was found rubbing shoulders in the salons of the France of Louis XIV, with remnants surviving in Europe despite various revolutions here and there and the growth of such democratic notions as "fair shares for all" and "Jack's as good as his master."

Among the masses in Australia, however, there is a very keen appreciation of leisure, there being no other country in the world, with the possible exception of New Zealand, where it is so difficult to find shops and businesses open after 5.30 weekdays or twelve o'clock Saturday morning.

And society, in the sense of overfed overdressed people with nothing to do, sitting around drinking and eating and talking frivolities, does exist in Australia. In fact, a cursory glance at the daily newspapers in each capital might give one the impression that little else exists. There they sit, transfixed in photo flash, the gilded coiffured dollies of café society and their tuxedoed males, like the denizens of some latter day antipodal Roman Empire in decline, whooping it up in never-ending bacchanalian rites before the vandal hordes descend from the north to finish it off.

Photographs with captions such as "Mrs Beth Bathurst, Mrs Di Davenport and Mrs Gloria Proudfoot, who before her marriage was the well-known model Janice Jewel, got together at lunch yesterday to discuss details for the forthcoming charity ball in aid of Unfortunate Swaggies," repeated ad nauseam in the columns of the daily press, generate an impression of Australian womenfolk as largely occupied in sitting around restaurant tables in flower-pot hats, talking tittle-tattle and boring each other to distraction.

In reality, however, away from the society pages of the newspapers, this is not the picture at all.

Ninety-nine per cent of Australian women, engaged in the tasks of child-rearing and home-minding, or going out to work to pay off the mortgage, never look into a newsphoto lens from one year's end to another. It is the one per cent who are doing it repeatedly who give this misleading impression.

A much more truly representative example of an Australian social evening than the evening dress and the bottle of chianti on the restaurant table would be the barbecue on the suburban lawn, the remains of the chops and sausages tidied away, the men in shirt sleeves clustered around the beer keg, talking gearboxes and clutches and differentials, and the women waiting to go home.

Australian society is essentially a four-wheeled society. Being such a big country, with not many people in it, it follows that the inhabitants are fairly well spaced out. Without a car to get you around, social life becomes largely a matter of staying on your own block.

The family car is not so much an extra, an indulgence, nor a status symbol, as a built-in feature of the normal way of life, like the fridge and the telly and the garden mower.

The biggest monthly hire-purchase payment of the struggling wage earner, after the house mortgage, is usually the payment on the car. He must have it in order to keep up the other payments, as it is usually his means of getting to work.

A working knowledge of what makes a car tick is part of the average Australian's mental stock-in-trade by the time he reaches his late teens. An appreciation of the differences between a camshaft and a con rod is much more widespread than, for example, the differences between democracy and dictatorship. A man incapable of getting out his spanners at the week-end, to take the head off a motor and change a set of piston rings, is generally held not to have much about him; to be a bit of a drongo, when it comes down to it.

Unless he lives on a bus route or near a railway station, the weekly workaday routine of the average Australian worker begins with starting up the car on a Monday morning. A busted radiator or a choked carburettor or a burnt-out coil presages a minor crisis; he is starting the week in a stricken condition.

An evening out for the family might well be a visit to a drive-in cinema, to remain parked for two or three hours, following through the windscreen the flickering images on the huge outdoor screen beneath the Southern Cross; or possibly a visit to a stock car rally to watch an assortment of bodged-up old bombs careering into each other as they race madly around the circuit.

With the five-day working week duly put in, the car

permitting, he uses it again on Saturday morning to run down to the TAB shop to put a dollar on the daily double or maybe knock back a couple of schooners with the boys in the bar.

Saturday afternoon he may well spend under the car, bleeding the brakes or adjusting the clutch plate or maybe just giving it a general greasing.

On Sunday, an outing to the beach or a bush picnic or visiting friends or relatives again depends on the all-important family transport.

In fact, it may be said that the internal combustion engine is the vital mechanism that keeps Australian society going. Without his car, the modern Australian male is like primitive man without his club or his spear.

Many male friendships have been dented, never to be fully restored, because of some offhand passing reference to "that smoking old rust-bucket of yours."

Australian men will argue the respective merits and demerits of different makes of cars with the same passion that men of other races reserve for arguments about the qualities of different women.

"The good old FJ, she was a beaut. They've never turned out another model to come up to her," a man will say with that touch of reverent nostalgia, as though recalling the one great love of his life.

Much has been said of the peculiar sexlessness, the inbred puritanism of the Australian scene; though whether puritanism derives from too little feeling for sex or too much is a moot point.

That shatteringly unfeminine America-derived phenomenon, the marching girls, in which young maidens decked out in uniforms step it out in ramrod military style behind the drums and trumpets in a travesty of demure maidenhood, something that has never caught on in Europe, is quite widespread here.

It could be that the striking uniformity of Australian culture, as manifest in the virtual absence of locality, has begun to permeate the sexual scene, as it were; that the women, weakened by the everlasting admonitions that this is a man's country, have, perhaps on some deep unconscious level, adopted the dictum "if you can't beat 'em, join 'em," to the consequent dilution of their sexual identity. This would account for the considerable numbers of Australian women who can run faster, swim farther and hit tennis balls harder than most of the men of other races.

Outback, a man's wife can still be referred to as "a longhaired mate," "mate" being used in the sense of matey rather than mating; the inference being that there are a few women who must be admitted into the hallowed brotherhood of Australian mateship.

Then the Australian accent is essentially masculine, in that it is much more likely to make a woman sound manly than a man womanly.

Native colloquialisms like "Stone the crows," and "Too right," fall strange from female lips. The Australian idiom just does not seem to have bred gossipy feminine-flavoured colloquialisms, like "Goodness me," or "Well I never," or "Oh dear."

One disgruntled English immigrant, intending to return to his wet drizzling native land on the first boat after his two years were up, tried to explain his lack of communication with Australia by saying, "There's something wrong with the women here. They're like these damn gum trees — this blasted sunlight all the time has drained some essential sap out of them."

This may have been an expression of some personal idiosyncrasy rather than a valid sociological observation of Australian womanhood; though there is a common complaint among single male immigrants that it is much more difficult to get "it" here than back where they came from, "it" being casual sexual intercourse.

Australia has yet to produce her Kinsey, and no authentic figures are available of the incidence of sexual promiscuity. Indeed, it is doubtful whether such a survey could ever be successfully accomplished here, as a normal Australian reply to such questioning would be "Mind your own flaming business." There would, however, appear to be far less canoodling and carrying on between couples in public places here than, for example, the parks of London or the metro in Paris; but again, the ubiquitous motor car, which may be described as a built-in adjunct to Australian courtship, must be taken into account.

There are no lovers' lanes here; no lanes at all, in fact, except traffic lanes. There are the bitumen highways and the red dirt roads winding off into the bush, and if a courting couple were to be seen walking along one of these it would be assumed, not that they were strolling through the countryside in the enchanting mists of love's young dream, but that their car had broken down and they were needing a lift.

Wolf whistling after any passing skirt is not nearly so prevalent as in Western Europe. In workers' smoke-oh breaks, while the occasional dirty joke does not come amiss, there is nothing like the same grinding monotonous insistence on the old fundamental subject at its crudest level that is found among corresponding company in Britain, for example; and even the British, by Latin tradition, betray a curious lack of interest where sex is concerned.

It is the dream of most high-spirited Australian girls to travel overseas before marriage, and see those exciting exotic places reeking with history that the travel brochures tell about. It is partly, of course, the general restlessness of the young that is found everywhere, particularly in an affluent society. But it is more so in Australia because this is so much a derivative culture, geographically isolated among strangers. It is not Djakarta, Bangkok, Delhi, or old Cathay that the young want to see before they settle down, but London, Rome, New York and Stratford-on-Avon.

One of the stock complaints of the bored Australian girl, pining to travel overseas, is that Australian men are boorish; that they are too wrapped up in their cars and beer and football and horses to pay the proper gallant courtesies that should be accorded young ladies.

However, after their European experiences of being ogled and whistled after on street corners, of having their bottoms pinched in public places by lustful Italian strangers and generally forming the opinion that the world west of Fremantle is peopled by a lot of sex maniacs, they are often

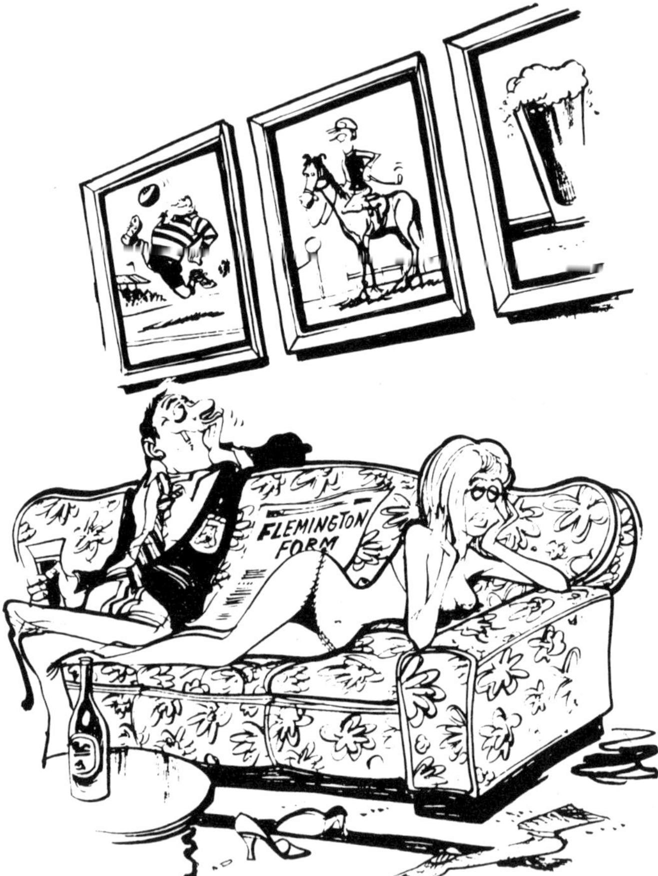
FLEMINGTON
FORM

quite pleased to return to the unconcerned Australian male, too wrapped up in the state of his sparking plugs or the tread on his tyres or what is going to win the 2.30 at Randwick to pay much attention to their new hair-dos or the swinging dresses they are wearing.

Perhaps some imperceptible shift of cultural evolution is at work here. It is essentially in the culture of the West, from the gallantries and the joustings of the mediaeval knights to the latest for-love-of-a-woman saga of Hollywood, that romantic love between the sexes, the old His and Hers dichotomy, looms with such towering significance, bolstered as it is now by the multi-million dollar entertainment and advertising industries. A nifty-looking blonde showing a shapely leg beneath a mini-skirt is used to sell anything from a packet of cigarettes to a motor car. "This girl gets attention because she has everything—and the same can be said of our slinky seductive irresistible eight cylindered torque transmission super de luxe model . . ." and so forth.

Could it be that the position of Australia on the map of the world, the proximity of Asia, is unconsciously exerting some influence on the embàttled Australian male, so that sex-wise, at any rate, he is slowly heeling over to an Oriental view of things, in which this matter of sexual attraction occupies a much more modest place in the general scheme of things?

Nevertheless, it is difficult to imagine any Eastern system of marriage by arrangement supplanting, in Australia, the Western idea of romantic love and marriage. We have not the time-honoured social ramifications nor the almost mystic regard for property of those peasant societies that go back in history a long time.

What would a suitable bride dowry be in Australia but a hundred cases of stubbies, or the like? Would the bride's father expect this of the groom, or the other way round, in the Australian context? Or would there be a mutual exchange? Two men exchanging identical gifts might be alright in Asia, where tradition and protocol count for so much, but in any foreseeable future in Australian society they would be "carrying on like a couple of flamin' dills."

Nor is it likely that any Asia-derived system of concubinage will displace existing institutions here, as the disposition of the Australian male is not towards more than one wife but rather to a certain lack of concern about having a wife at all.

What may evolve here is the growth of marriage by arrangement within the existing fabric of our society—i.e. through the marriage bureau and the growing multiplicity in the personal columns of the press of such items as:

> Healthy young Australian male would like to meet sheila willing to give it a go in wheatbelt town 250 miles west of Sydney.

The use of the word "sheila," as a blanket synonym for any nubile young female, is indicative of the casual playing-it-down attitude of the Australian male towards sexual attraction.

More revealing, semantically, is the use of the shortened "darl" for his beloved in place of the old English word darling, which is too fancy, too flowery, coming it a bit thick. "Darl" is warm, matey, egalitarian; free of any suggestion of boudoir slop. A fellow would feel a right nong coming out with something like "When are we going to eat, darling?" But "Shake it up darl, where's the tucker?" is the way you would expect a hungry bloke to speak to his sheila.

The present sexual temper of our society must be seen against the country's historical past, for the greater part of which men greatly outnumbered women, and here we may refer to that classic work, *The Relevance of Sex to the Australian Situation*, by Professor Chas. Gilbey, Head of the Faculty of Sexology, U. of A.: "In a society where wives are scarce and strumpets know their value the obvious solution for the frustrated male is to adopt the pretence that sex is not as important as it was previously held to be.

"Whether it was a case of the pretence, once adopted, being found to be nearer to reality than was supposed or of being held long enough to assume the weight of conviction, the fact remains that sex does not command the importance here that it does in societies that historically have been more liberally endowed with womenfolk.

"Even after the ratio of the sexes evened up here, a certain imbalance persisted, indeed persists to this day, in that women are found to have a predilection for the creature comforts and more equable conditions found on the coast, whilst the mining and pastoral sectors of our economy demand some dispersal of the population inland.

"In fact, one might say that the role of women in our history has tended to be not to be there at all or to an uneven distribution of themselves when they are there, so that today, viewing the woman-starved outback and the overwhelmingly male communities of places like Mount Isa, Weipa and Mount Tom Price, one cannot but wonder whether some form of mobilised harlotry might not be an appropriate element in our social situation."

Professor Gilbey goes on to see our prowess in sport as a direct result of sexual deprivation: "The game of cricket is largely composed of unrelieved periods of tedium suddenly broken by ear-piercing sub-literate yells of 'Owzat,' accompanied by frenzied leapings and gyrations with arms outstretched when the stumps — an obvious phallic symbol — have been knocked down." (See Appendix II — *Cricket as a Form of Sexual Compensation.*)

Alienated from the romantic in Western sexual culture we might be, but there is as yet no sign of alignment with the East in the sense of sublimating our sex drives in ideology. There are no local variants of the Red Guards, nor can the imagination visualise the day when hordes of Australian youths will go rampaging through the streets of Sydney or Melbourne chanting inane political slogans like "Act big — vote Lib" or "It's fab to vote Lab," and thrusting booklets of Thoughts of Premier Billy (or Chairman Gough) on to unsuspecting passers by.

Could it be, in fact, that with his darl-and-sheila syndrome the Australian male is slowly groping, albeit on some deep subconscious archetypal level, towards a working norm, some *modus vivendi* of the sex urge, as it were, between the sex-mad West and the sexless East: that he is having a go, giving it a burl, playing it cool, doing his own thing somewhere between the frenzied juvenile youth-worshipping bosom-fixated razz-matazz on the other side of the Pacific, the West in decline, and the frightening humourless zombie-minded leader worship to the north, the East waking up?

It has been said that should sex be declared illegal in Australia, this would cause less of a furore than, say, a ban on the sale of alcohol, the closing of TAB betting shops, or politicians voting themselves another increase in salary.

This must remain a matter of conjecture, as the repressive measures of social legislation of the past, though quite formidable in volume, have never included this particular prohibition.

It must be remembered, however, that we live in a democracy, and should the circumstances arise whereby some political mileage would appear to be promised by such a prohibition — a pendulum-like reaction, for example, to the contemporary permissiveness in sexual matters — there is no saying what proposals may be brought forward for legislation, and we will leave the final words on this matter with a quotation from Professor Charles Gilbey's classic work *The Future Co-Existence of Man and Woman on the Australian Continent*: "The deep sexual polarity of our society has been remarked upon too often by outside observers for us to pretend it is not there. Time and again the European visitor to our shores has recorded his astonishment at the various social gatherings he has attended at seeing the mutually exclusive congregating of the men and women at opposite ends of the room.

"While this self-sufficiency, this apartness of the sexes, remains confined to the formal social occasion, no harm will be done: indeed it will remain a quaint, some might say bizarre, but an authentic indigenous trait of Australian society to impress the visitor from overseas; but should it extend to the more intimate areas of living—from the salon to the boudoir, so to speak—then the future of our society, whether as a bastion of Western European culture in the South Pacific, or as an outlying but integral part of Asia, or indeed as anything at all, will be in the gravest jeopardy, for without some measure of fruitful contact between the sexes no earthly society can carry on for long."

5

THE CULTURE HANG-UP

A nation's image must amount to something more than surfboards and meat pies. If the Sydney Opera House did not exist it would be necessary to invent it.

MINISTER FOR CULTURAL AFFAIRS

In an egalitarian fair-go do-it-yourself democracy like Australia the fundamental point of interest about a bloke is what does he do. If the answer is that he is a poet or a painter, the puzzled reaction is, "Yeh, but wisecracks aside —what does he *do*?"

The idea of a man making a living writing books, maybe writing books about blokes who write books, is definitely a bit rum. Music is generally taken to be the Hit Parade, the Top 40, as presented in never-ending assembly belt fashion on commercial radio by the pacesetting pattering disc-jockeys; those crazy swinging deejays, man. A painter is assumed to be a tradesman in the building industry, a man in overalls with a ladder. As for the other kind, daubing bits of colour on to canvas, making pictures women like to hang up in the lounge, as like as not of something you don't know what he's on about — well it's not the sort of thing a dinkum Aussie gets up to. And as for theatre — well, what's that but a mob of poofters skiting around in fancy clobber?

In fact, the mass feeling for the arts here is very similar to that in other literate affluent neo-Christian western societies.

It is just that in such a thinly populated homogeneous outdoor society as Australia there is that much less of a minority inclined the other way.

The clean spacious cities of Australia have no Left Banks, where blokes with beards live in attics and get by without going out to work every morning or paying union dues or taking out insurance policies. There are no bars or restaurants where they sit up till all hours of the night drinking wine and going on about the human condition. By ten-thirty p.m., 89.2% of the Australian population outside of Kings Cross are in bed.

There are no inbred literary circuits where the weekly reviews are discussed at great length. The week-end is the time for the trek to the beach or the bush, with bathing togs, snorkels, fishing tackle, transistors and a few beers in the cold box; the weekly hedonistic pilgrimage to the great outdoors.

Who would want to be bothered about the dilemmas of civilisation in a climate like this?

It is only the day before yesterday that the land was pioneered, and, by the rise-and-fall graph of civilisation, Australia is still very much on the rise line, with a generally outgoing practical self-reliant temper and not much in the way of art galleries, concert halls or gourmet restaurants.

In the early days, those with the time and the inclination to straighten their backs from the mechanics of living to try to give form and expression to what was going on in Australia, tended to look around this strange untamed land with an air of loss and nostalgia, as though looking for the sights and sounds of another place.

> *Oh kookaburra why do you laugh*
> *And England so far away?*

— might be described as the theme line of some of the early poets.

As things became more established, there was an awakening realisation that what was *here* was different to what was over *there*. As the Australian-born began to express themselves, there was a vigorous reaction from expatriate lamenting to the assertion of an independent nationalistic spirit.

> *Give me the roo and the mozzie,*
> *The beaut sheilas in the surf;*
> *And put me down as an Aussie,*
> *The salt of the flamin' earth*

— became more the general tone of things.

A certain maturity has now been reached; an awareness that what matters about an Australian poet is not that he is an Aussie, but what he is like as a poet. An array of sophisticated critics now lies in wait to shoot down any bard who comes along with only the smell of gum leaves in his hair to recommend him.

Young Australian artists and intellectuals flock overseas if they can afford it, to drink first-hand at the wellsprings of Western culture. Some stay on, expatriates in the London fog or amid the Grecian ruins; most return to make their peace with the saltbush plains and the weatherboard suburbs. To the steady unimaginative centre, such comings and goings are very much a fringe activity. "Most of that mob would be displaced persons anyway mate."

The great flowerings of the arts seem to have occurred in times of great social inequality, in countries where the national culture is old, and these conditions have not existed in Australia. There are stinking rich here, like anywhere else, but no wealthy, leisured, dilettante class. Wealth tends to be acquired rather than inherited, and the fellow who has made a million is not much good for anything else by then except making another million. He would die of boredom if he stopped working, and sees no reason why he should squander his wealth on keeping a mob of dreamy good-for-nothing no-hopers writing verses and painting pictures.

The sort of millionaire who makes a fortune out of selling breakfast cereals or manufacturing bathplugs and then, possibly under the influence of a charming actress wife, discovers Art and begins to dispose of his millions by encouraging young artists is a very rare, one might say non-existent figure, on the Australian scene.

"It is a sad and irrefutable fact," reports the *Annual Culture Review*, "that over-rich Australians, when they do choose to divest themselves of some of their surplus wealth by indulging in non-commercial activities, are much more likely to breed racehorses than establish poetry foundations." (The Arts in Australia : Is there any Hope? Vol. II. Quarto IV.)

As for popular patronage of the arts, short of introducing some competitive sporting element such as a knock-out Poet of the Year tournament, with the rival bards declaiming against each other, there seems little prospect of any dramatic upsurge of interest from this quarter. The chamber music recital, the exhibition of abstract impressionism, the performance of Japanese Noh drama, however faultlessly presented, simply do not rate, attendance-wise, against the beach, the drive-in and the stadium.

It is held by many Australian artists, compelled to work as wharfies, ringers, shearing shed rouseabouts and plumbers' offsiders in order to go on eating, that Australians generally are the most aggressively philistine people on earth, that they have an in-built hostility to the creative, the original, the beautiful, and would like to see all artists packed off to a reserve in the Northern Territory or somewhere.

This is something of an over-statement, an understandable reaction of the personally embittered. The general attitude to the arts is one of indifference rather than hostility: if a fellow wants to have a go at being a sculptor or a poet or a 'cellist, good on him. But if he cannot make any money at it he will have to go out and work for a living like the rest of us. It is the concept of art as something beyond entertainment, something deserving of subsidy by the state, that the average Australian taxpayer cannot or will not comprehend: that is where he jibs.

This phobia that the rest of the population is against him, that he is neglected, unrecognised, without support from the powers that be, is characteristic of another figure in our society often associated with the artist: the intellectual.

This class is difficult of definition at any time, particularly in Australia, where nobody has ever been known to admit to being one, at any rate in public: but it is generally assumed that they are there somewhere, and "the intellectuals in our society" is an accepted concept in contemporary dialogue about the general state of things.

"The contention that the intellectuals in our society are not given the support and recognition that is their due," writes Bradley Winterhof, Research Fellow at the Ballarat Institute of Sociology, "is one that is frequently made, but is found to be made invariably by intellectuals themselves, and it is difficult to delineate here between valid objective criteria of the social structure and mere indulgence in the great national pastime of whingeing." (*Whither Australia?* B. Winterhof, University of Australasia Press.)

Under the auspices of the Institute, Winterhof made a nation-wide survey of the attitudes of the public towards intellectuals, and comes up with some interesting figures. 7.9 per cent, it seems, approve of intellectuals. 6.4 per cent would like them turned out of the country, if possible. While 83.9 per cent replied 'Don't know' to all the questions put to them.

"In this, as in so many other fields of social enquiry," writes Winterhof, "it would appear that the uncertain shapes of the future are going to be determined by the Don't knows."

Replying to recent accusations of anti-intellectual bias in government circles, the Minister for Cultural Affairs said that it simply was not true that import quotas had been set for intellectuals in our immigration programme. They were as eligible for assisted passage here as bricklayers and boilermakers, and why they did not come here in appreciable numbers was no doubt due to the fact that, by and large, they felt more at home in Europe, where things generally were on the decline, than they would in a young vigorous up-and-coming society such as ours.

"These men," said the Minister, "thrive on picking holes, finding fault, going on about what is wrong in society, and have the good sense to realise that if they come to a lucky country like ours, where there is very little wrong, they will find it that much harder to practise their talents.

"As for the intellectuals who are here," the Minister concluded, "both imported and home-grown, I can give them my solemn assurance that the majority of my colleagues in the cabinet, far from bearing them any animosity, do not even know they exist."

In a recent government report commissioned by the Treasury on the advisability of making further grants to the arts, it is stated: "Whatever it is the arts are about, the way they go about it awakens no interest in the vast majority of the population, and if the democratic tenor of our society is to be preserved this is a cardinal factor to be borne in mind in any formulation of government policy."

Over the whole field of relationships between the State and the arts looms the gigantic spectral shadow of the Sydney Opera House, which some say has put back the cause of State encouragement for the arts at least fifty years. How many young promising Australian poets and painters of the future are doomed to languish and go hungry in attics and crumbling basement flats in Wollomolloo and Paddington and Fitzroy, for lack of government support because of the traumatic effect of the Opera House fiasco, will never be known. What is known is the remark of one prominent politician to another: "If we can only get it into the heads of the electorate that the opposition is thinking about building a couple more opera houses, we're home and dry at the next election — at every election for the next ten years."

It was back in the 1950s, oh so long ago, when we were a young confident prosperous outgoing society lighting out for culture, that the fateful decision was taken: Sydney would have an opera house. If it was not the biggest, then certainly it would be the best in the world. A responsible judging panel was formed and the challenge was thrown out to architects the world over: show us your best, your dreams of an opera house. Down here is a government ready to make them into reality.

Notice was being served on the world that we were a provincial backwater of cricketers and kangaroos and koala bears no longer; that we had arrived. We were going to have an opera house that would turn them green with envy in places like Milan and Salzburg and old Vienna.

Furthermore, by one of those strokes of genius extremely rare in public administration, it was decided to pay for it all by a series of lotteries, thus enabling the Australian to continue his mania for gambling while going his bit for culture at the same time. It may be asked in passing why the government does not use this form of revenue-raising more often, in order to pay for other things just as expensive and of even more doubtful social value than opera houses, such as battleships and swing-wing jet bombers, thus leaving the conventional spending power of the country for such matters as schools and hospitals and low-cost housing.

But to return to the Opera House story. The designs were chosen, the man came, the project got under way. The years passed, the costs soared and nothing was completed. A perfectionist was at work. "The most flaming perfect perfectionist in history," a Sydney alderman was heard to mutter. "And with our flaming money."

As the original estimate of five millions escalated to ten, fifteen, twenty, thirty, forty millions, so the misgivings grew. This sort of money was not peanuts, even by government standards, even if it was being raised by gambling. Could even Australians go on gambling at a rate sufficient to pay this lot off?

The suspicion, ever present in the minds of some, that these artist blokes never know the value of money, that they will spend it like water, particularly when it is not their own, gathered weight. The knockers became more vociferous in their accusations.

Tensions grew; personalities clashed; words were spoken. "What are we supposed to be building here — Fort Knox or the Parthenon?" "Well, make up your mind! What do you want — an opera house or a honky tonk?"

Too much money had now been spent for the whole thing to be bulldozed into the ground and the idea declared a non-starter. The question was whether to cut our losses, and turn a few Aussie carpenters and plasterers, well versed in our she'll-be-right-mate tradition, loose on the job to finish it off quickly. Or, as things had gone so far now with money apparently no object, rather in the style of the pharaohs and caliphs of old, to let it be carried through to a finish in the same grandiloquent manner, to see what we got at the end of it: a thing of beauty, where nobody counted the cost.

In the midst of all this, the man whose original conception it had been departed; whether voluntarily or otherwise was not clear. Other, some would say lesser, men have taken his place. The work continues, and there, for the moment, the matter rests.

To quote from a recent hard-hitting book on the subject *The Sydney Opera House: Fact or Fiction?* by A. K. Drott, a well-known Sydney journalist: "After all the mud-slinging, the bitterness, the intrigue, the calling of names and, not least, all the money down the drain, what have we got?

"We have something unfinished, the only building in history to become a ruin before it was finished, and which, to finish now, could be nothing but an anti-climax.

"We have got what we deserved. Let it stand forever by the harbourside, a mute and eloquent testimony to the tragic folly of an essentially materialistic society going in for the culture stuff."

Perhaps the one good thing to come out of all this has been the making of that masterpiece of the Underground Cinema, *No Birth of a Nation;* a film shot wholly in Australia, under Australian direction, with an all-Australian cast; never shown on the commercial circuits and obviously inspired by the Sydney Opera House story.

It tells of Gaelene, an intelligent romantic high-spirited Australian girl, engaged to Ron, trainee accountant, league prop forward, scuba skin diver, dragster racing driver. The mood of our outgoing affluent lucky society is confidently established as the young lovers surf and dance and go places together: the souped-up Holden Monaro roaring along the newly-constructed expressway; meat pies and saveloys and dim sims in late-closing milk bars run by courteous monosyllabic Greeks in darkened outlying suburbs; bathing in the nuddy on moonlit beaches while the transistor wails soothingly amid a welter of snorkel tubes and flippers and king-size filtertips; the crash of racquet against ball; the spumey foaming of surf against bronzed body, and the all-pervasive, sensuous, almost pagan background of sea and sand and sun and surf and sky.

It is a good life and Gaelene knows it. Yet she cannot help feeling there is something missing, and she realises what it is when she meets Axel, a brilliant European architect who has come to Australia to design a concert hall for Sydney's North Shore.

Axel is sophisticated, sensitive, complex, artistic, introverted: all the things that Ron is not. He finds Australia captivating: he says he is fascinated by the light, by the sense of youth and the future. He visualises Sydney as an

NOW SHOWING
NO BIRTH OF A NATION
MUM
Monaro
MADE IN AUSTRALIA
GUNDAGAI
UNDERGROUND
CINEMA

Athens of the South Pacific. This sort of talk only brings out the boorish and resentful in Ron.

In a dramatic confrontation between the two men, Ron says, "Look mate — if you like Athens so much there's a travel agent's down the road where you can get yourself a ticket. This is Sydney, Australia, and if you don't like it here why don't you shove off?"

Speaking slowly through clenched teeth, Axel replies, "You are an antipodean boeffel."

Sensing this is something uncomplimentary, that he is, in fact, being called some Balt version of a drongo, Ron rushes forward, but Gaelene intervenes and the two men never speak to each other again.

Axel's plans for the concert hall are seen to be costing too much money, even for North Shore residents. The clodhoppers, the zombies, the hatchet men gang up on him. He is given concrete where he wanted marble; breeze blocks where he wanted concrete; fibro where he wanted breeze blocks. Finally, he tears up the plans on which he has laboured so long and walks out.

He says he is going to look for a still more backward society where things have not yet been corrupted, where it will be possible to create in a climate of innocence, and asks Gaelene to go with him.

But meanwhile Ron has paid cash for a perch block out in the western suburbs and is spending every week-end building a brick veneer house with patio and barbecue unit.

Gaelene's choice between the two men is not revealed, and this is artistically and beautifully correct. The film closes with some magnificent panoramic shots of the Harbour and a final zooming close-up of the concert hall, scamped up and finished and converted to a rollerdrome-ice palais-wrestling-stadium.

Relationships between artists and intellectuals on the one side, and politicians on the other, tend to be rather prickly at the best of times, at any rate on this side of the Iron Curtain. In Australia, this state of affairs is exacerbated by the censorship restrictions, the authorities responsible for which are being constantly lambasted as faceless philistine ogres, set upon keeping the Australian public in a condition of benighted cultural provincialism, and this could have some bearing on the degree of encouragement given by the state to the arts.

Politicians, after all, are only human, and if you refer to them as bird-brained inhibited power-drunk Victorian prudes, completely out of touch with the contemporary scene, then you can hardly expect them to turn round and give you money, even though it is not their own, so that you can put on something by, say, Samuel Beckett or Bertholdt Brecht.

The Australian imagination would appear to be essentially pictorial rather than literary, inasmuch as there is far more awareness of what Superman, Batman and other epic heroes of the comic strip are up to than of what writers like Joyce, Miller and Lawrence had to say about the human condition. Australia is possibly the only country in the world outside America where one might see at a service station a man in a big expensive car unselfconsciously absorbed in a kids' comic as he waits his turn for a fill-up at the bowser.

Such literary censorship prosecutions as come to court are more likely to be over ephemeral girlie magazines than serious works of literature.

With the latter it is more a matter of trailing in the wake of English sensibilities. If they have been accepted over there, then they may be allowed in here after a respectable margin of time has elapsed.

Generally, the tolerance level of censorship, literary censorship at any rate, would appear to be somewhat above that of Ireland and below that of England. Apart from intellectuals and customs officials, there is a feeling among the populace at large, inasmuch as they are concerned at all about such matters, that pornography is some kind of European ailment that, like chilblains, you do not have to worry about in this climate.

It is the Protestant syndrome that prevails here; the numerous liquor sale prohibitions, the depressing hotel bars, the near-nudity on the beaches, the undergrounding of prostitution, the generally quiet dull loiterer-free city streets at night.

In fact, about one-third of the Australian population is Roman Catholic, and though the Catholic understanding is associated with a more accommodating view of the wine, women and song side of man's nature, little of this influence has broken through on to the Australian scene.

Australian Catholicism is held to be of the Irish parochial stamp, not bothered much with intellectualism: though the overwhelming Irish derivation, with the consequent, within the context of Australian history, anti-English and anti-establishment leanings, has given it, politically, a surprisingly radical stance by Western European comparisons.

There have been predictions of some leavening of the Presbyterian-Baptist-colonial-what-not bleakness of the Australian cultural scene through the large scale immigration of Southern Europeans; volatile back-slapping Greeks and Italians with weird habits like eating on the pavement outside the café instead of inside, and not liking meat pies, and strolling through the streets at all hours of the night. And indeed, there are Australians now who know their wines and take an interest in exotic foods, and gourmet columns are sprouting in some sections of the Australian press.

It is doubtful, though, whether such decadent influences will spread much beyond certain cosmopolitan quarters of the big cities.

Those Italians who leave the cities, to sweat it out among the sugar cane stalks and the grape vines, are far from being the fun-loving opera-trilling fellows of popular imagination, who like nothing better than to lie in the sun swilling the vino. They are usually from hardy peasant stock, and work such hours as to make an honest Australian unionist head for the nearest bar in disgust.

One cannot imagine any Southern European cultural influences having much effect in those harsh sun-scarred back blocks, where fundamentalists of various persuasions go round of a week-end explaining some passage from Saint Paul's Letters To The Ephesians to anyone who will stand at the door and listen, and where you might see, stuck on the broken-down gate of some independent battler, a notice like JEHOVAH'S WITNESSES — KEEP OUT.

Rather it is the immigrants who will be absorbed; whose sons will grow up knowing more about pumping engines and old utes and tractors than ever they did about wine and ravioli.

Perhaps the most striking feature of Australian culture to European eyes is its homogeneity, its lack of regionalism. Given that there were no Middle Ages here, no village greens, no centuries of generations living and dying without going beyond the parishes of their birth, but white society has been established in Australia for nearly 200 years now, long enough, one would have thought, for some regional diversity to develop.

Yet there remains one Australian accent, one Australian sense of humour, one Australian audience. Such diversities as exist are those between the educated and the less educated: the bushwhackers and the urbanised; the teenagers and the oldies; the swingers and the squares.

The generation gap first appeared in Australia in 1960, midway between the advent of television and the arrival of the Beatles.

Up till then, while the Asian pattern of extreme respect

and veneration for age had never had much influence here, some sort of dialogue between the young and the adult had been possible, was indeed traditional, even though on a basis of mutual grudging tolerance as between "these boring grown-ups who think it's still as it was in their day" and "these youngsters of today who think they know it all and will not be told anything."

But with the advent of the guitar, shoulder-length hair, and the electronic pop group, the lines of communication between the generations broke down completely. The shutters were put up, and with expressions like "Drop dead dad, you've been around too long" and other cryptic utterances from their newly-minted argot, the young in our society served notice that henceforward they were strictly on their own — but for real, man.

Far and away the best analysis of the Beat Scene in Australia is *The Teenage Thing and the Cultural Predicament*, by Walter Fluke, Reader in Social Semantics at the Ballarat Institute of Sociology.

Fluke produces convincing statistical evidence to demolish the popular supposition that the teenage cultural explosion is directly related to the newly-established teenage affluence, and writes: "In the late 1950s, when the Beatles were in chrysalis on Merseyside, as it were, unemployment in Liverpool was running at an overall annual rate of 8.9 per cent, whilst in Melbourne at that time the annual unemployment rate was as low as 1.3 per cent, and youngsters there were enjoying an affluence they had never known before. Yet no Yarra Sound, no local counterpart to the historic Mersey Sound, was produced of that time and place: though it may be mentioned in passing that in the coffee bars of Melbourne in 1963 a group could be heard, consisting of a girl singer and three "dinkum Aussie" male guitarists, which, in a few short years, under the name of The Seekers, would shatter forever the world myth that the Australian male was incapable of handling anything but an axe, a cricket bat or a tennis racquet."

To get to the aetiology of Beat, Fluke maintains, we must dig deeper than economic prosperity: "Expensive quiffy hair-dos, fab gear and shining electric guitars are but the trappings, the accoutrements of this dynamic force. They do not explain the dynamism itself, which is something to do with the chemistry of youth: its zing, its dash, its rip-roaring and iconoclastic irreverence. And, as such, its sexual undertones are fundamental."

Beat, as Fluke defines it, is the language of the inarticulate, a statement about life by the conceptually indifferent: It is the expression of those who want to go but who do not know where they are going, of those who have not yet arrived and have no intention of doing so — and who exult in the very mindlessness of their vitality. For any baffled adult over the age of twenty-five to begin to understand what is being said behind the wild and frenzied shakes and gyrations, the screaming and the hypnotic strumming, he must first understand that this is for those to whom mortgages, superannuation, the lawn mower, the RSL, the ACTU, the Australian Lawn Tennis Federation, the Victoria Trade & Labour Council, Ansett Airways, the Melbourne Cup, the Bank of New South Wales, the Parents' & Citizens' Association, BHP Pty Ltd, the Wool Exchange, the Stock Exchange, the annual Commonwealth-States financial conference, Advance Australia Fair and all the accepted stabilisers of western urbanised man in the South Pacific are 'strictly for the birds', so to speak. It is a statement at once of insecurity and affirmation."

There has always been a strong element of mobility in Australian society, far more so than in any European country. The idea of "shooting through," of "giving it a go" in some other place, runs strongly through working life, particularly among the single and unattached. Even families with several young children, with a roomy car or station wagon and a few pots and pans and blankets, moving around from place to place, settling in at a caravan site for a year or two, are not uncommon.

Mining communities are essentially of limited duration. When the ore is worked out the mines close down and the workers move on, leaving a ghost town of crumbling shacks on the empty plains.

Even Australian farming has not the same degree of settled father-to-son pattern of more fertile countries. Proportionately, more farmers go bust through drought and pest, give it away, and go to work for wages, than possibly any other country in the world. Even if the farm remains a paying proposition, then the isolation, and concomitant lack of educational and job facilities for a growing family may well cause a farmer to sell up.

Then the astonishing growth of mass communications in recent years has militated against any development of regional culture. Each capital city has its own morning and evening dailies, combining news and views of world affairs with daily jottings on the local social whirl and the sort of small print advertising of jobs and of houses, businesses, budgies, piano accordions and other miscellaneous articles for sale more associated with the local weekly press in the United Kingdom.

But there is now also a national newspaper, *The Australian*, which combines serious reviews and articles on religion, education and the like with a regular astrology column and a comprehensive guide to TAB betting.

Does this indicate that the sort of Australian who is informed on the dilemmas of UNO, aspects of the ecumenical movement, the possibilities of dialogue between Catholic and Communist, also takes an interest in whether he is Aries or Taurus and likes to have a dollar each way on the tote? The matter awaits statistical investigation.

The main purveyor of culture is the Australian Broadcasting Commission, and the only cultural diversity from this source would be between those who work in broadcasting and those who do not; a sort of enclave characterised by a tendency to grow beards and drink wine as against an essentially clean-shaven and beer-drinking normality.

The A.B.C. is modelled on the B.B.C., attracting the same cosy inbred "dear old auntie" tag; drawing its revenue from the licence fees of the populace but leaving the commercial stations to cater to the lowest common denominator of public taste.

The programmes include school lessons and religious services, drama from Greek to kitchen sink, music from pop to classics, a comprehensive world-wide news coverage and discussions on pretty well everything from the way to cook cauliflowers and cashews to the agnostic's concept of God.

Free to comment, but liable to take off programmes whose comments offend the establishment, the A.B.C. carries, as the *Cloncurry Times* puts it, "the flaws and the virtues inherent in the institutionalisation of mass communications under the aegis of the State."

With the advent of television the cultural uniformity of Australia has been sealed and cemented. Not only is Queensland culturally indistinguishable from Western Australia, but both are rapidly becoming indistinguishable culturally from Warwickshire (United Kingdom) or Nebraska (United States of America). *The Man From U.N.C.L.E., The Saint, The Lone Ranger, Peyton Place, Coronation Street, Skippy, Lassie* and *Yogi Bear* have planetary coverage.

Culture, in the sense of something communicated to an audience, has, in television, found the medium to reach the masses; the most important cultural milestone since the printing press.

Such art galleries, theatres and concert halls as there are in Australia remain unvisited by, indeed largely unknown to, the populace at large. But apart from a few outlying areas "back o' Bourke," the number of Australian homes where the telly is not on for a couple of hours of an evening grows fewer year by year. And even in the Never-Never, costs of erecting television transmission stations in places like Darwin, Mount Isa and Hughenden have already been quoted by the Postmaster General. With television, in fact, we are dealing not with coterie audiences but with the bulk of the population.

There are four channels in Australian television; three commercial and one non-commercial, the latter run by the A.B.C.

The A.B.C. channel relies heavily on programmes

previously run on the B.B.C., while the commercial channels rely more on American imports to supplement the staple diet of old movies.

A typical evening's viewing on a commercial channel would be a western feature, a crime feature, an old movie, a situation comedy—all American—and possibly a panel game, the idea taken from overseas but using Australian personalities.

On the A.B.C. there might be a comedy, a documentary and an episode of a drama serial—all from the B.B.C., with perhaps a sporting or farming feature of Australian content. Most programmes that make any impact on the B.B.C., and which are not of exclusively British interest, are eventually shown on the A.B.C.

With one lot relying too much on American programmes and the other on British programmes, the old cultural cry is raised—what's wrong with the local do-it-yourself Australian stuff?

Is it a lack of imagination in high quarters that will not give Australian talent its head?

Or is the Australian capacity just not there; is the human element, essential for successful television production, something which is peculiarly lacking in the Australian character?

Or is there no demand for the local product, the preference of the viewers being for the more finished professional stuff produced overseas?

The A.B.C. channel, which is the main standard-bearer for Australian production and which carries the more serious and varied programmes generally, runs consistently below the commercial channels in the viewer ratings, and this despite its freedom from the commercials themselves; those endless insistent jingly snippets telling of the ultimate whiteness achieved by various toothpastes and detergents, of the car with the velvet touch, the beer with the foamiest top, the cigarette with the dreamtime flavour, the sort of soup to give Him when he comes home tired from the office, the kind of chocolates to give Her when she thinks you no longer love her, the furniture, gadgets, appliances you must possess to be with the people who live at the rainbow's end, and how to deal with halitosis, headaches, constipation, indigestion, insomnia, nervous tension and various other ailments that human flesh is heir to.

To unload this lot night by night into carefully allotted time-slots, and still capture the big majority of viewers, would seem to indicate that most viewers have an inexhaustible capacity for being advertised to and prefer the sort of programmes the commercial channels go for, the smooth, professional, guns-glamour-gags entertainment that America turns out with assembly belt efficiency. The drift of television, for all its intimate living-room impact, is not to the local, the homespun, the amateurish, but to the slick admass products made for world-wide distribution.

In such a packaged form of entertainment industry there must be a tendency for the best in the business to assemble where the money and the resources are available. Once a television programme is shot and in the can it is a marketable commodity.

With further improvements in satellite communication it might be possible for Australian television producers to go out of business altogether as viewers here sit back and enjoy programmes bounced across the oceans of the world.

This Anglo-American hang-up over the Australian scene extends far beyond the field of television. In such a derivative culture the need was to assert identity, to proclaim independence; "Anglo-nothing, mate — Australian!" With such rough-and-ready beginnings this came naturally to the man-in-the-street, or rather the man-in-the-bush. He was his own man from the start. But to the small number of Australians given to musings on things like the cultural heritage, the central dilemma has been trying to discover what being an Australian really means, and many cloudy words have been written on this cloudy subject.

The law, the political constitution, the education system were all derived from Britain. How many generations of Australian schoolchildren have sat in weatherboard schools set in the sun-scorched gum-scented distances, dutifully learning by rote poems about cuckoos and green meadows and fields of yellow corn?

That essentially English institution, the public school, or rather private school, is a built-in part of the education system in Australia; though they are virtually all church schools, as though it were felt necessary, in such a levelling godzone democratic society, to have the sanction of the Almighty for such class-breeding privilege-festering institutions as fee-paying schools.

But time and distance have had their effect. However derivative the social institutions, however selective the immigration programmes — and until post-war years nearly all the immigrants were of British stock — 200 years of living in a large empty continent in a dry sunny climate south-east of Asia, instead of in a small overcrowded island in a cold wet climate north-west of Europe, must make for something different; and the weakening of the pull and influences of the Old Country has been greatly accelerated in recent years by the shifts of power on the world political scene.

But as the Anglo influence has waned, the American influence has strengthened. American whalers were the first foreign vessels to call in Australia, way back in the early days, doing a brisk trade in rum and other commodities, when the country was still a struggling prison farm around Sydney. But it was not until the 1920s, when the Hollywood movies began making their impact, that there was any dramatic increase in Australian-American contact.

It will be for historians of the future to assess the true cultural significance of that suburb of Los Angeles in the second quarter of the twentieth century. In the meantime we may refer to that minor classic of social analysis, *The Influence of Hollywood on the Australian Outback*, by Carl Ottomeyer, in which he writes: "It was through the cinema screen that the Australian stockman, or ringer, came to realise that his opposite number in the U.S.A., known as the cowboy, had become a great national mythic figure, and it has been suggested by various Marxist thinkers on the subject that the erection of movie houses across the Australian interior, composed as they are of galvanised sheeting that could well be surplus fencing material from the great grazing properties, was heavily subsidised by the wealthy pastoral companies in an attempt to induce the stockman to see his job in a new light and thus reduce labour turnover, the Australian stockman being a man prone to "shoot through to the coast," to use the parlance, "and get it easy with the rest of the bludgers there on a 40 hour week."

Be that as it may, the long-term effect of the moving picture on our pastoral industry might be other than anticipated, as was demonstrated by a recent incident at one of the less remote cattle stations where television reception became possible, in which the stockmen refused to go out on mustering camp as it would have meant their missing episodes of *Wagon Train* and *Laredo*, claiming that watching television was the only social amenity available to them owing to the isolation of their working lives.

This "group narcissism syndrome" of television, as it has been called, whereby viewers are really viewing themselves doing something, or rather what they themselves would be doing if they were not viewing television, would play havoc with the national economy should it spread to all sectors of the community, as a man who spends long enough viewing dramatic presentations of his working life soon ceases to have a working life of his own. He becomes stricken with what, for want of a better name, we may call 'tellyitis'; a phenomenon already known on the domestic front, as can be testified by those unfortunate husbands returning from work to find the house neglected, no dinner in the oven, and the wife "glued to the box," as it were.

Side by side with the cultural seepage, not to say saturation, from America via the telly, there has been heavy investment of American capital into the newly-discovered mineral wealth of Australia, which strengthens the dark misgivings felt by some that "the Yanks will be running this place soon."

Then the Australian background itself, with the frame bungalows petering out into the wide unfenced spaces, the spread of the small country towns along the one main drag, the drive-ins and parking lots and fill-up stations, is much more akin to the American scene than the British.

In an interesting recent work on this subject, *The Pacific Ocean: The Dwindling Pond* by S. F. Crook, the author writes: "Taking a jet from Sydney to San Francisco becomes ever more less like travelling from Point A to Point B than like travelling from Point A to Point A."

American scientists and meterologists returning from a working spell in Antarctica are always being quoted, upon arrival in Australia on their way home, as saying how they more or less feel at home already.

It may be held, of course, that after a year or two of seeing nothing but snow and penguins, anywhere else would appear like home upon arrival. But it is significant that the latest American to express these sentiments, saying how good it was to be back home in America, was, in fact, still on Australian soil, his America-bound jet from Sydney having been re-routed back to Townsville owing to weather hazards over the Pacific whilst he had been sleeping.

Of course, Australia is not the only country where Americanisation has proceeded apace of recent years. Who does not want to belong to the consumer society if it means you consume more of everything? Where America stands today, consumer-wise, the rest of the world hopes to stand tomorrow. The ad-man cometh with seven league boots and the car-fridge-telly syndrome girdles the earth.

But for the custodians of Australian culture, the impact of American influence, coinciding with the waning of Anglo influence, gives ground for a special just-as-we're-getting-shot-of-one-lot-we-get-another sort of resentment.

"Look at this pacesetter," says the men's wear commercial on the telly. "With a suit like that you would think he had just stepped off the last jet from London or New York. But he hasn't. You can buy swinging gear like this without leaving Australian soil. Call at your local fancy-pants store. Today."

Or again, an airline commercial. "Go to London. Stop off and see San Francisco's Nob Hill. See New York turn on. Go to London. Swinging ringing ding-a-ding London. Where it's all happening. Now."

A load of old codswallop, of course, and the Australian has as sharp an eye as any for codswallop. But beneath the ad-man's mush is a residue of reality.

The cultural heartlands are over the sea. Polynesian we will never be except in geographical location. We inherit no easy pre-literate rhythms of lying in the sun, waiting for the bananas and coconuts to ripen. For better or for worse, our heritage is Western European, with all its attendant guilts and aspirations, and as such we are a far-flung outpost at the end of the sea lanes and air routes.

Over there are the great metropolitan centres of our language and culture; over there is where the new ideas clash and ferment, where the new styles and trends and fashions originate. "Skirts in London are two inches down this season," or "In Paris now the bosom is out," the fashion correspondents report back to the Australian scene with due respect.

In the early days of the mini-skirt, when a London model appeared at the Melbourne Cup races with her skirt several inches above the knee, she received more attention than the horse that won the Cup, and in Australia you cannot make a bigger impact than that.

The trip overseas, perhaps for two or three years, to get the feel of things in Europe, and now, as well, or perhaps alternatively, America, bestrides the enquiring young Australian's dreams like a colossus.

And it is against this sense of isolation that the native indigenous plant must develop; as indeed it has. There is now a growing body of painting and literature that could have come from nowhere else but here; the Australian experience made manifest.

And yet, and yet . . . the knockers are heard in the dovecotes. Have we sloughed off the old smothering Anglo influences, the Town Halls redolent of nineteenth century England, the mandatory roast beef and Yorkshire pud when it's ninety-five in the shade outside, the genuflexions towards Buckingham Palace and Westminster Abbey, the lingering traces of Victorian respectability, the provincial airs of a far-flung outpost of the imperial realm — only to emerge as a satellite of the American age?

In the quiet corners well away from the neon-lit muzak-droning supermarkets, the drive-ins and the hamburger bars and coca-cola signs, where the twos and threes gather together to discuss the cultural well-being of the nation, the uneasy misgivings are raised — are we, in fact, becoming a sort of fifty-first state, a kind of trans-Pacific Texas, even though a flaming sight bigger?

6

THE MYSTIQUE FOG-UP

Australia is a legend in search of its own reality.
　　　　　　　　　Professor O. D. Bunkhoff
　　　　　　　　　"Where Do We Go From Here?"

If we are going to get anywhere with a discussion on mystique we must stop being mystical about it and come down to facts and figures.

99.9 per cent of Australians have never run a mile in four minutes, nor won the lawn tennis championship at Wimbledon. 98.4 per cent have never been attended by the Flying Doctor service nor spoken to their neighbours on bush radio. 97.8 per cent have forgotten when they last said "Stone the crows, my old cobber, are you fair dinkum?" 96.5 per cent have never killed a snake. 78.2 per cent have never swung an axe. 69.3 per cent cannot ride a horse. 48.4 per cent have never seen a kangaroo in its natural habitat. 56.7 per cent have never seen an emu at all. And virtually 100 per cent of the Australian-born never speak of the United Kingdom as "Home" any more, if indeed they ever did.

So much for the overseas image of the Australian as a tough leathery stock-booted axe-swinging bushwhacker. To be fair, it is an image that is not confined to overseas; it is something that a lot of Australians like to delude themselves with. Napoleon meant it as no compliment when he referred to the English as "a nation of shopkeepers," and it would be doing no good for Australian-Chinese relationships were Mao Tse Tung to refer to us as "a nation of suburbanites."

The fellow catching the 8.15 every morning, adding up figures all day or clocking in for a stint at the factory belt, mowing the lawn at the week-end and paying off mortgage and insurance policies, is not the stuff of which national myths are woven, and is not an impressive representative figure for a rugged outdoor society such as ours is supposed to be. Somewhere in the national psyche is the feeling that it is the bush that has forged us the way we are, even though we may only visit it for the occasional week-end picnic.

One of the most heavily urbanised of nations we might be, but you would never guess it from our folklore. It is the bushie, the man from farthest out, the man with the aura of the outback about him who shoulders the myth of our collective identity. On the rare occasions when, fortified with beer and fellowship, sentiment overcomes our sardonic reserve and urban inhibitions to the extent that we burst into song, we sing, not of frustrated wage-earners seeking an escape from the forty hour treadmill through alcohol, but of "the jolly swagman who camped by a billabong."

Apart from the bush, the other great natural feature contributing to the outdoor mystique is the beach, with the surfies waiting easy in the sun for the perfectly breaking roller, and the lifeguards, with their inter-club competitions and pageantries of bronzed husky young men, wearing skull caps vaguely reminiscent of Russian moujiks, marching in formation with pennants flying across the sand, and rushing like lemmings into the waves.

If the dry dusty unyielding bush is the setting for the legendary Australian at work, the golden surf-ringed beaches are the setting for his play.

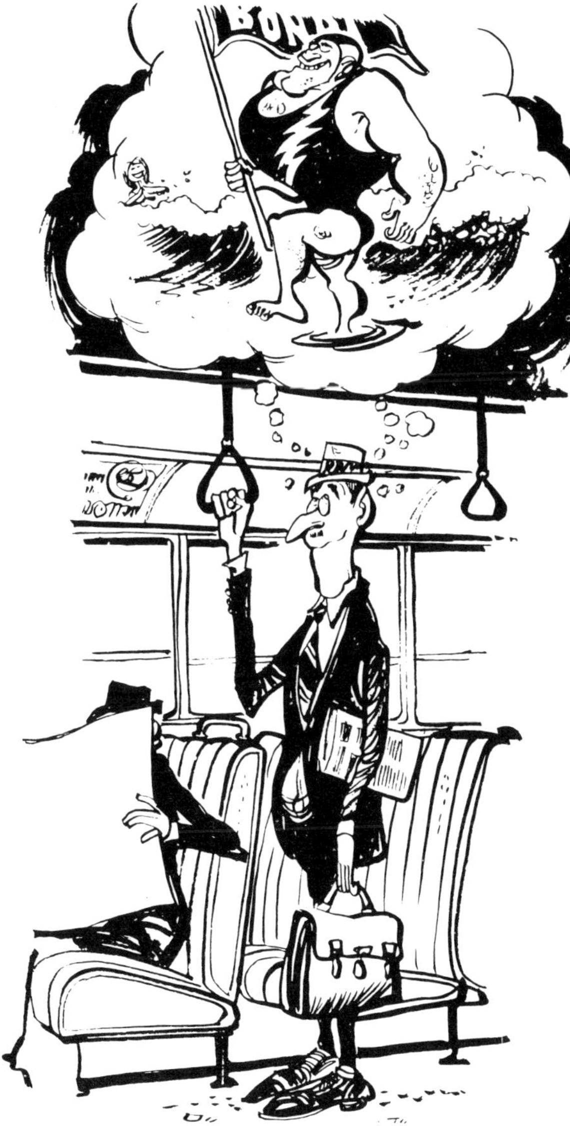

The hedonist and the puritan are uneasy bedfellows in the Australian character. The point of life is not chasing success but enjoying yourself, and yet by no reckoning is this the permissive society.

The so-called "wowsers" are strongly entrenched, with their restrictions on gambling and drinking. Along with the overall free-and-easy casual mateyness, the absence of tipping and cap-touching flunkeyism, there are unexpected conventions like obligatory collar-and-tie in unlikely places, drink lounges where men are not allowed without women, the bars where women are not allowed at all.

Women coming here from Europe are often surprised at the conservatism of dress and style of Australian women, though this does not apply to the teenagers, whose styles and trends seem to know no frontiers.

While a lot of men go through the sunny week-ends barefooted and in rumpled shorts, on working days white shirts and ties are *de rigueur* for most office and technical staff.

Some overseas observers who come for a quick look around and stay long enough to observe where most of the people live, exclaim, with an air of revelation, "But they live in suburbs!" and go on from this to see our dilemma as being sort of sunburnt Englishmen *manqués*, lost in an alien land, trying rather pathetically to reconstruct Slough-on-the-Pacific or Croydon-by-the-Bush.

But if they stayed a little longer to ponder a little deeper they might arrive at the not so subtle conclusion that it came to be thus because of the way things were; that the way people live is largely shaped by the sort of place they live in; and that most Australians live in towns, not because of any atavistic yearning for a lost suburban heritage, but because Australian soil has never been fertile enough to support large numbers in agriculture, and grazing properties do not carry much labour.

There has been nothing here to compare with the American West, no exciting expansionist decades of the interior being opened up, no covered wagons with their loads of women and children and pots and pans and the future rolling out for the frontiers, as it was realised early on that there were no unending prairies beyond, with the waving grass knee-high; only a lot of flaming old salt bush and spinifex.

The frontiersman here was not so much a trail-blazer, breaking through for the rest to follow, but rather a fellow battling to hold on, often giving it away to go back to the coast to work for wages. The barren sun-scorched distances stamped that wry sardonic battling look on the Australian face a long time ago.

At no point in Australian history is it conceivable that the young ever got advice similar to that classic piece from American folklore, "Go west, young man, and grow up with the country."

The North, of course, is our equivalent to the American West, and any advice given on this matter here would much more likely be on the lines of, "Go north if you want to finish up on the grog like the rest of the no-hopers up there."

Heading for the Alice or Darwin has none of the air of going out to build the future: rather of "shooting through" from the present; of "giving it away." The empty boozy North is for those who want to get away from bus stops and postmen and milkmen and newspapers and women, the hard cases who find it too overcrowded within a thousand miles of Sydney or Adelaide or Brisbane.

The Australian frontier called for men with capital, for government assistance, for collectivism. The scale was too big, conditions too harsh, for the struggling smallholder. Against such a stark and inhospitable environment men had to band together: the lonely spaces bred the cult of mateship.

It was never a land for a peasantry. Along with a hardy self-reliant individualism and a marked distrust of authority went an acceptance that state action to aid development was inevitable. Today, in the sparsely-populated outback, a sizeable proportion of the few living there are government employees of one sort or another, working for the Main Roads Department, local government, the railways. The Australian railways were state-owned from the start.

There was none of the American paranoid suspicion of government action as the thin end of the wedge of the creeping paralysis of socialism: no fear of socialism anyway. Australian rural workers were the first in the world to organise themselves into a militant union.

There was no tradition of an ordered hierarchy, of "the rich man in his castle, the poor man at the gate" as being the rightful order of things: no class of "our betters."

Those with the land and the money had got them by various forms of skullduggery. When the battle to "unlock the land" was finally won in the nineteenth century with the Selections Act, whereby the small man with no money and no connections could get a grant of land, he found all too often, alas, that without any capital he could not make a go of it; that he was better off working for wages. Today, the fellow with a few acres, whose dream is to work his own land and be his own boss but whose reality is to work for wages through the week and be a farmer just at week-ends, is common enough.

There is an air of false promise of an easy living about this wide empty sunny land. When the gold strikes came, for every one who came back rich from the diggings a thousand sweated to scratch enough to keep on sweating. Too many have toiled and bullocked here for nothing, beaten by drought or pest or glut, for the Australian to swallow the tale that the rewards of this world go to those who work the hardest.

Worldly success is what you might get if you are lucky, but you are more likely to get it if you are wicked.

There is nothing exactly wrong about getting on: but just doing an honest job and having good mates alongside you is better.

Not that a lot of Australians would not opt to be millionaires if they were given the choice. The recent minerals boom, with the soarings and fluctuations on the share market and a growing awareness among the bulk of the populace of the Stock Exchange as some sort of outsize TAB betting shop, only paying better odds, a place where it is possible to make large sums of money for doing nothing while remaining within the law, has led to widespread share buying by any number of small investors, hoping to make a catch in the fishy waters of high finance.

In a nation-wide survey conducted under the auspices of the Ballarat Institute of Sociology, to the question "Is money important to you?" the overwhelming majority replied "My oath," "Too flaming right" and in similar emphatic affirmative terminology, while 12.3% did not give a direct answer, their various replies being to the effect that anyone who did not know the answer to that one knew nothing about anything in our society. Of the .2% who replied in the negative to the question, most were employed teaching philosophy and similar disciplines at the universities and were drawing comfortable professional salaries with annual earnings well above the national average.

But for all that, in the national legend the man who gets rich by his own efforts carries no shining aura: in fact, he is much more likely to be a bit of a crook, while it goes without saying that the man who is rich by inheritance never had the chance of making an honest start.

The big boss is somebody to be distrusted, somebody to stand up to, rather than somebody to be emulated. There is no Australian version of the log-cabin-to-White-House legend; no fibro-shack-to-Government-Lodge dream success story to spur on the battlers. Any bloke taking that road would be turning his back on his mates, and to get that far would mean he had to be something of a pusher, with a pretty shrewd eye for the main chance.

In the Australian ethos there is nothing wrong with mediocrity; nothing sparkling about élitism. The mob here is not the rabble or *canaille*, but a bunch of regular blokes.

The philosophy implicit in the Australian legend is that what life is all about is not proving yourself the greatest, the best of the bunch, except in sport of course, or burning yourself out to make a million, but just doing your whack, getting what enjoyment you can, a few beers, a bit of fishing, being one of the blokes, and not expecting any pie-in-the-sky because the whole show is run by a pack of con men; always was and always will be.

The temper is stoic rather than Christian. There is no hangover here from the Middle Ages; long centuries in which there was not even the vocabulary to question belief in God.

Whatever godless road swinging England may be set upon now, some residue from the past still lingers there. The church bells can still summon the faithful to worship in village churches, even if hardly anyone under thirty is going any more.

But here the Age of Faith was never known. From the start this was more of an uncloistered humanistic air, where man was pitted against the bush and could cherish the simple hope of being happy by his own efforts; or at any rate he could stand by his mates and take stoically what was coming.

The conclusions that some disillusioned thinkers seem to arrive at in middle age — that power corrupts, that the wicked shall flourish like a green bay tree, that no good can come from those in authority, that the trappings of the high and mighty are just a load of bull — are something that the Australian starts out with and carries around undisturbed unless he is stricken by conversion, or maybe elevated to high office himself.

The socialism that promised here was no blueprint of intellectuals but a simple rough-and-ready banding together of blokes to stand up for their rights against the boss squatters: an extension of mateship.

Much water has flowed under the bridges since then, and now that the trade unions themselves are such monolithic organisations the grass roots have withered. The simple earlier hopes and intentions have long since faded in the rot of organisation, the back-biting and intrigue attendant upon the election of union officials as upon that of presidents of state, and the overwhelming apathy of the masses concerned. Many unionists hold their membership reluctantly, because there is no choice about it, and are more prone to whinge about the unions than the bosses. Indeed, when union dues are increased, as they inevitably are by the executive without the mandate of a popular vote, a strike against the union could well be on the cards were there any organisation to bring it about.

Things are never run by a good bunch of blokes in their spare time from doing an honest job of work, if for no other reason than that the blokes are much more interested in what is going to win the 2.30 or where the fish are biting than in the way things are run.

Ideas as such have no great currency on the Australian scene. Egalitarian the country may be, but the gap between workers and students is just as yawning here as it is anywhere else.

"I never thought it possible," says Kev Pinkerton, brilliant ex-radical student leader and now brilliant advertising executive, "to find in Australia another body of men as reactionary, as narrowly sectarian, as unimaginative, as monumentally boneheaded as the United Wool Graziers' Association — until I went to a meeting of the Australian Council of Trade Unions."

Trade union leaders tend to be middle-aged men with arid legalistic minds, cagey wary guardians of vested interests, much better informed on what Para. II, Clause IV says about sickies and doctors' certificates than on what thinkers like Shaw, Orwell, McLuhan, Marcuse and that lot have to say about things in general. Engaged largely in lawyer-like manoeuvrings over the finer points of arbitration techniques and industrial awards, they are much more akin to the shrewd hard-headed bosses they are ranged against than to young student rebels hot in the pursuit of grand intellectual concepts: whilst the mass of the workers themselves are as little inclined to get excited by the clash of ideas as they are to attend the boring minute-taking Trades Hall meetings of their unions.

In a revealing book on trade unions entitled *The Australian Labor Movement: Why I Gave it Away*, by Cec. Blunt, an ex-shop steward, the author writes, "The normal attendance at the monthly Trades Hall meeting, covering the interests of several thousand union members, was 11, consisting of 8 shop stewards, 2 full time union officials and 1 rank-and-file member who did not drink, did not like the telly, and could not stand the company of his wife of an evening."

Inasmuch as there is any popular conceptualising about the sort of society Australia should be, then it is for the society that gives a man "a fair go," a concept that is held to be self-explanatory, not needing any further elucidation.

If a bloke is getting a fair go, then there is no better goer in the world than an Aussie, runs the legend. But if he is not getting a fair go, he can hold his own with any as a shovel-leaner.

One of the worst insults is to call a man "a bludger," a fellow who is not doing his whack, who is leaning on his mates.

"I won't bludge" says the hard-up canecutter in *Summer Of The Seventeenth Doll* to his barmaid-mistress, who wants to shout the drinks until the sugar season starts up again.

The suspicion that other sectors of the community are composed largely of bludgers is widespread. The farmers see the townsfolk with their bitumen roads and 40 hour weeks as bludging on the primary industries, the townsfolk see the well-off graziers as bludging on the sheep, whilst by general consent the biggest bludgers of the lot are in the government, running the show.

A motion by the extreme left-wing faction of the Victoria Trades and Labour Council to have the office of Governor General re-designated as Bludger General was defeated only by the narrowest of margins.

The best you can say about a fellow is that he is "a battler," a term involving all the instinctive Australian sympathy for the underdog.

"25 acres for sale. Dam, fencing, good soil. Would suit battler," runs the advertisement, presumably inserted by someone who has had enough of battling himself.

Though the term has traditional rural connotations—a bloke battling to wrest a living from the hungry Australian earth, who drives a rattling old ute to market with a few boxes of beans or pumpkins he has sweated to grow, to find the market glutted—it can be used of anyone who is up against it; a fellow whose wife is sick, whose job has no future, whose home is needing repairs he cannot afford; the eternal underdog. But he does not let it get him down; he battles on. The battlers are the men who will never be rich, never be successful, never be on top; but they are the ones who carry the rich and the mighty on their backs.

In such a relentlessly anti-heroic climate, it is no accident that the one authentic hero of Australian folklore is Ned Kelly, the Victorian outlaw, coming out to face the waiting guns of the cops in a pathetic home-made suit of armour. He had the requisite trappings for Australian heroism; of Irish emancipist stock, the family struggling to make a living on the land, on the wrong side of authority from the start.

So much has been talked and written around the Kelly legend that the facts are now obscured in a mist of conflicting hearsay and scholarship. Was he a fine shot, a great horseman and bushman, as game as they come? Did the cops keep picking on him? Was his sister wronged by a copper? Was the Kelly gang betrayed by a despicable informer?

Or was the Kelly family a loud-mouthed braggart nogood Irish clan, full of the blarney? Was Ned a ruthless delinquent, a rough-neck horse-thief in trouble with law and order as soon as he was old enough to make a nuisance of himself? And now, one of the more recent accusations, of all the dirty lowdown things to say about a bloke — was he homosexual?

The debate shows no signs of resolution.

Facts are not so important in the creation of a legend, and at this point in time perhaps the most fascinating point of all is why the legend gripped, why it took root.

Australians generally do not read history books once they leave school, and if a population-wide census were taken now to name one famous dead Australian the odds are that the name that would dominate would be Ned Kelly, bushranger and cop-killer, strung up in Melbourne Jailhouse, 11 November 1880.

The typical Australian as defined by mystique seems to turn out a pretty mixed-up character. A suburbanite convinced that the best come out of the bush, a rugged individualist at home in the conformist mores of urbanised society, a man who loathes a bludger whilst holding that only mugs die of overwork, with an ingrained distrust of authority, but bored by intellectual abstractions and the play of ideas.

And this contrariness, this conflict of conclusions about the sort of fellow he is, is in keeping, because the Australian is not impressed by any fancy theorising that has it all cut-and-dried.

There is a great tradition of improvising; making do. This is the land where a fellow was out on his own, with no experts to tell him, and found out as he went along by having a go. And the suspicion of anything doctrinaire remains.

Theories might be all right in places like Canberra, where they don't do any proper work. But when there is a real job to be done it is the goer spirit that is needed, not fancy theories and textbooks.

The bush carpenter may not have his apprenticeship papers, but he will have a roof over his head while the fellow who just knows it all in books is still sorting out his tools.

The profession that commands respect far in excess of all others is that of medicine. The doctor has to have brains to get through college and everything, and the job he does at the end of it is worthwhile and has to be done. The medical profession may be as zealous as any other in its pursuit of monetary reward, but this does not take away the aura it has of being more selfless and admirable altogether.

In more primitive societies the holy man and the medicine man were often one and the same person. In a modern westernised society like Australia, with no rooted religious past, the doctor, with his mysterious lore of knowledge about the human body, seated in his cloistered surgery dispensing scripts for pills and potions in his weird indecipherable scribble, seems to have gathered to himself some of that veneration traditionally accorded to a priesthood.

To try to summarise these various traits and echoes of legend and ethos, let us endow this mythic Australian bloke with a few workaday features.

He would essentially be a man of the land, and the farther off the tramlines the better, with a wayward sympathy for bushrangers and possibly two or three years medical training.

He would, of course, be struggling, overdrawn at the bank, though working a sight harder than the bank manager, and forced to go and work for wages when things were really grim, the drought going on too long, or the bean fly and mildew ravaging his crops.

Working for wages, he would certainly do his share alongside his mates, but would not bust a gut working for any boss. He would pay union dues if asked, but would never be a union official. Unimpressed by pomp and worldly splendour, uninterested in questions about why we are here or where we are going, disposed to friendship but nobody's fool; all in all, a dinkum disenchanted sort of bloke, forever battling to give it a go in the land of the fair go.

7

THE FUTURE

When Asia sneezes, Australia has convulsions.
OLD CHINESE PROVERB

Australia was founded on the assumption that the British Navy would be around for always, ruling the seas; that the British Empire was a more or less permanent feature of the way this world was ordered, and the fact that this is no longer so means that Australia is lumbered with something she never had before — a foreign policy of her own.

A new breed of diplomat has arrived on the South East Asian scene, speaking Cambodian or Mandarin or whatever it is with an Aussie rather than an Oxford accent, and sending his reports of how he sees the local situation to Canberra, not London.

The British withdrawal from east of Suez has left something called "a power vacuum." Perhaps if such vacuums were encouraged to grow, to expand until they coalesced and the whole world became one power vacuum, it might be the end of our international troubles. But this is to think contrary to all established canons of diplomacy, by which these power vacuums are danger areas, places into which you must get your foot before the other fellow gets his.

Thus, when the British moved out it was hoped that the Americans would move in.

The Yanks, like the Poms, have their faults, but by and large they are our mob. They speak our language, albeit in a funny sort of way, but we understand what they are going on about. We have similar political institutions; we pay lip service to the same values. Our attitudes to God, sex and marriage are interchangeable. Their TV programmes are just as bad as ours; some of our worst, in fact, are theirs.

Americans, however, are considerably more intelligent than their TV programmes might lead one to suppose, which may be a contributory factor to misunderstandings in the East-West confrontation generally.

At any rate, they are quite capable of working out where their vital interests lie without any assistance from us. Their leaders are there to act in accordance with the wishes of the American electorate, not with the requirements of Australian foreign policy, and they have learnt to be very wary of commitments in Asia.

It would appear that there will be no all-embracing Australian-American alliance to give us the sense of security once known within the protected realms of a mighty empire. Yesteryear is down the drain for ever. When the chips are down we could be all on our own, expendable from the viewpoint of every government except the one in Canberra.

This calls for a drastic reorientation of national attitudes and a belated but final acceptance of just where we are on the map of the world.

It is one thing, however, to say we are at the crossroads and quite another to indicate which road we should take.

Here we are, prepared to mind our own business, intending harm to no one, with no dreams of territorial aggrandisement against anybody; is our future not secure without looking into the lunacies of international affairs?

A look at the past, however, shows that minding their own business is precisely what the Aborigines were doing when we came along. If history teaches one thing it is that being a threat to nobody is no guarantee that nobody is going to threaten you.

We inhabit a largely empty continent off the teeming lands of Asia, and at the heart of the Australian dilemma is the great unanswered question of the White Australia policy.

Sixteenth century Chinese coins have been found on the North Australian coast, which would seem to indicate that the Chinese discovered this land before we did, but did not fancy settling here. What they thought in the sixteenth century, however, is not necessarily the same as what they are going to think in the twenty-first century. Sooner or later, according to some, we must open our doors to Asian immigration; to be a multi-racial society is our destiny.

But to come down from historic destinies to brass tacks is to get lost in the mist. Even the most rabid opponents of the White Australia policy do not suggest that we start $20 assisted passages for emigrants from places like Calcutta, Singapore, Djakarta, Hong Kong, Peking.

What is suggested is permission to enter for Asians capable of assimilation into the Australian way of life; skilled and professional people — precisely those, in fact, whom the emerging societies of Asia would appear to have most need of themselves. It is the coolie multitudes, the underfed masses, who are most in need of a place in the sun.

Just what optimum population can comfortably be carried by Australia has never been settled with any general measure of agreement.

According to some, it will be time very soon to call a halt to the immigration programme, regardless of creed or colour, because of our uncertain water resources.

Estimates of experts as to an optimum population appear to vary between fifteen and fifty millions, as do the estimates of those who are not experts. The huge mineral deposits that now give Australia's future such an expansive glow will not be there for always. Mining is essentially an activity of limited duration, as the ghost towns testify; and mining operations, anyway, are now so highly mechanised that comparatively little labour is required.

That this will always be a comparatively empty continent,

in fact, would appear to be decreed by nature. There is a limit to what technology can do, and the Never-Never would have filled up long before now if there had been any easy pickings there.

Indeed, there are those who hold that anybody mug enough to think he can make a living out in the spinifex should be made welcome to it, regardless of where he comes from: but an immigration programme conditional upon the immigrants staying "back o' Bourke" is not practicable.

Perhaps this bugbear of the White Australia policy will finally be laid not by any action of any Australian government but by the recent revolutionary advances in methods of birth control. Who would want to leave the fertile paddy fields and head for the mulga scrub if the paddy fields were not overcrowded?

Problems of living space and immigration aside, the question of relationships with Asia remains to dominate any formulation of an Australian foreign policy.

In a situation so fraught with difficulties, it is held in some quarters that the best policy is a non-policy, that where the best of intentions may go awry it is best to have no intentions at all, and the politicians responsible should make fewer speeches about what we are going to do when we really do not know what to do for the best. No cards should be shown at all until we know what is on the table. The whole business should be played by ear, so to speak.

Playing it by ear, however, is an essential part of politics at any time. If a non-policy is aligned to non-objectives, then the reasons for the very existence of the Department of External Affairs start to look shaky.

"What are those bludgers doing there anyway—why don't we close it down?" might well be the rumbled demand.

The changes in the international power structure in this part of the world have been so drastic in recent years that Australia's position might be compared to that of a family moving into a new district. What do we do about the neighbours? Do we keep our distance or do we get involved?

Then what does getting involved really amount to in practice? Behind these sonorous well-rounded phrases like "strengthening our ties of friendship and mutual regard with our Asian neighbours" what is implied?

Offers to teach them how to play tennis and cricket, or goodwill visits by bevies of Miss Australias and Meter Maids, with gifts of boomerangs and koala bears and bearing placards with messages like "Greetings from Your Cobbers Down South" will butter no parsnips.

No doubt Asian languages will come into increasing prominence in the syllabuses of the high schools and the universities, possibly at the expense of French, German and Latin, while trade with Asia, which has increased in recent years, will continue to do so if the supply and demand are there. Business, after all, is run on a basis of self-interest and no bones about it, and if we can find markets in Asia to replace those lost in Europe then no doubt any necessary ideological accommodations will be made. If China wants our wool and wheat and, in the mysterious ways of international finance, can pay for it, and we cannot sell it anywhere else, then there is not so much choice about it.

Civil aid programmes are often cited as a field where we could do much more, with references to remote statistics like one per cent per annum of the national income which would appear to touch on nobody's private pocket.

Poverty is not unknown, however, even in our affluent society; not poverty like Asia's, but then those struggling in Australia do not compare themselves with the struggling of Asia, but with those they see around them who can afford all sorts of things for themselves and their families that the strugglers cannot. Old age pensioners and those numerous families battling to make ends meet week by week may well contend that if the Australian government really has got any wealth to spare, it should start handing it out nearer home for those struggling to cope right here.

There remains the vital question of a military presence or otherwise on the Asian mainland. Should we maintain a squadron here, an armoured unit there; a mere drop in the ocean of Asian manpower, but mobile and mechanised brushfire forces to give a hand in the suppression of any guerrillas or subsersive groups we judge to be a threat to our interests? Or do we fall back on Fortress Australia; pull up the drawbridges and not get involved?

Asia is, after all, a number of sovereign states with varying degrees of stability and no end of disputes between themselves. The squabbling and bickering that go on at our State Premiers' conferences are as sweetness and light compared with the sort of arguments those Asian states get up to between themselves.

Should we stay out of it altogether? And how do we rate as a self-sufficient bastion in the South Pacific?

To quote from Brigadier Rod Rudd, brilliant Duntroon graduate and our leading military strategist: "Australia is not a part of Asia, and it follows from this that any invading force would have to cross water to get here. Our coastline is very long and cannot be guarded adequately if sufficient manpower is not available. However, if our coastal cities were made impregnable, any invading force could be left to penetrate to the interior, the aridity and desolation of which would provide a ready-made scorched earth strategy. The enemy would ultimately be defeated by the logistics of supply and communication, possibly in the Simpson Desert or on the Nullarbor Plain, depending upon where the beach-head was established and which route was taken."

If military strategy was ever a lot of stunningly boneheaded platitudes wrapped up in jargon, the nuclear bomb has made it irrelevant as well.

Professor Jolly, in his *Statistics of Overkill*, writes: "America now has a nuclear fire-power capable of wiping out the earth's population thirty times over, while Russia could do so fifteen times over. Bearing in mind our proportionate production potential, it is not beyond the capacity of Australia to produce a nuclear armoury capable of wiping out the earth's population once over, and as man can die but once and nobody can be deader than dead, this would put us on a par with the great powers, and questions of man-power become irrelevant."

Could we really be up there in the big league, and what would be the point of it? Would it mean an extension into Australia of the nightmarish hair-trigger confrontation that is said to exist elsewhere, behind the sinister secrecies of the super-powers? Would we have a fleet of nuclear bombers on a twenty-four hour alert, ready to take off and blast *them* off the face of the earth, if we thought that what we saw on our early warning system was not a wandering flock of galahs, but *them* coming to blast *us* off the face of the earth?

The future was ever uncertain. Is it becoming unthinkable? What is to be done for the best?

The politician who says he does not know what to do is in the wrong trade. That something will be done is for sure; though, all things considered, perhaps it were better, were it possible, not to do anything at all. As Professor Bunkhoff says in his classic treatise *Who's Fooling Whom?*: "The essence of statesmanship is to drift helplessly on the tide of history whilst pretending that you have compass bearings and good steering gear."

Anyway, if the madmen triumph and the button is pressed and this earth is reduced to a smouldering radioactive cinder, maybe, out on the old Barcoo or somewhere out west, there will be a survivor, a lone battler to emerge from his timber-and-corrugated shack, look out across the ruined planet, roll up his sleeves and roll himself a smoke, and say, "She'll be right, mate."